CCEA GCSE
AN INTRODUCTION TO PHILOSOPHY OF RELIGION

Revised Specification

COLOURPOINT EDUCATIONAL

© Paula McCullough and Colourpoint Creative Ltd 2021

Print ISBN: 978 1 78073 208 4
eBook ISBN: 978 1 78073 334 0

First Edition
First impression

Layout and design: April Sky Design
Printed by: GPS Colour Graphics Ltd, Belfast

All rights reserved. No part of this publication may be reproduced, stored in a retrieval system or transmitted in any form or by any means, electronic, mechanical, photocopying, scanning, recording or otherwise, without the prior written permission of the copyright owners and publisher of this book.

Copyright has been acknowledged to the best of our ability. If there are any inadvertent errors or omissions, we shall be happy to correct them in any future editions.

Page 81 constitutes an extension of this copyright notice.

The Author

Paula McCullough has taught CCEA GCSE Religious Studies for over 30 years in Methodist College, Belfast. She is also a senior examiner for an awarding body, and author of a number of textbooks for Colourpoint Educational.

Colourpoint Educational
An imprint of Colourpoint Creative Ltd
Colourpoint House
Jubilee Business Park
21 Jubilee Road
Newtownards
County Down
Northern Ireland
BT23 4YH

Tel: 028 9182 0505
E-mail: sales@colourpoint.co.uk
Website: www.colourpoint.co.uk

This book has been written to help students preparing for the GCSE Level Religious Studies specification from CCEA. While Colourpoint Educational and the author have taken every care in its production, we are not able to guarantee that the book is completely error-free. Additionally, while the book has been written to closely match the CCEA specification, it is the responsibility of each candidate to satisfy themselves that they have fully met the requirements of the CCEA specification prior to sitting an exam set by that body. For this reason, and because specifications change with time, we strongly advise every candidate to avail of a qualified teacher and to check the contents of the most recent specification for themselves prior to the exam. Colourpoint Educational therefore cannot be held responsible for any errors or omissions in this book or any consequences thereof.

CONTENTS

Chapter 1: THE EXISTENCE OF GOD — 7
The meaning of the terms theist, atheist and agnostic 7
Arguments for the existence of God 9
The debate between creationism and science about the origin of the universe 18

Chapter 2: THE NATURE OF GOD — 27
Ways of understanding and describing God 27
Contrasting beliefs about the nature of God 33

Chapter 3: THE PROBLEM OF EVIL AND/OR SUFFERING — 37
Natural suffering and moral evil 37
The origin, nature and purpose of evil and suffering 38
The challenge presented by evil and suffering 42
The teachings of world religions on evil and suffering 46

Chapter 4: EXPERIENCING GOD — 49
Ways in which believers experience God 49
The nature and importance of revelation 55
Examples of revelation 57
Challenges to religious experience 62

Chapter 5: LIFE AFTER DEATH — 66
The teachings of world religions on the afterlife 66
Non-religious views on the soul and the afterlife 71
Possible 'proofs' of life after death 72
The impact of belief in the afterlife 76

GLOSSARY 78
INDEX 82

INTRODUCTION

EXERCISES

There are various exercises throughout the book to aid learning. They are labelled with different icons:

ACTIVITY
These exercises are designed to improve skills such as thinking, problem-solving, decision-making and being creative.

IN A GROUP
These group exercises are designed to encourage group participation and debate. They aim to improve skills such as communication and working with others.

FURTHER THINKING
These extended exercises are designed to encourage research and wider learning. They aim to improve skills such as using ICT, self-management, managing information, thinking, problem-solving and decision-making.

QUESTIONS
These are examples of the types of question that could be found on a GCSE exam paper. They aim to test knowledge, understanding and evaluation skills. These skills can be identified by the trigger or command words used in each question:

Knowledge

There are two types of knowledge questions in the examination. In the book they appear inside a yellow box:

1. Short answers worth 1 mark. They usually begin with one of the following words:
   - Who…
   - What…
   - Name…
   - Which…

2. Short paragraph answers worth 5 marks. They usually begin with one of the following words or phrases:
   - Describe…
   - Outline…

Understanding

These questions require short paragraph answers (of about 10 lines) and are worth 5 marks. They require an explanation and appear in a blue box. They usually begin with one of the following words:

- Explain…
- Why…
- How…

Evaluation

There are two types of evaluation questions in the examination. In the book they appear in an orange box:

1. Short paragraph answers (of about 10 lines) worth 5 marks. These questions are open-ended and take the following wording:

    - "[A statement]" Do you agree or disagree? Give reasons for your answer.
    - Do you think… Give reasons for your answer.

2. Extended paragraph answers (of about 1 page) worth 10 marks. These questions are open-ended and take the following wording:

    "[A statement]" Do you agree or disagree? Give reasons for your answer showing that you have considered different points of view.

These questions require a response to the statement or question and are asking for knowledge and understanding to back up the evaluation (own opinion). You can respond positively (agree) or negatively (disagree); or combine both positive and negative points. It is the quality of the argument that attracts marks rather than the viewpoint adopted.

KEY TERMS

These boxes include useful explanations of the key terms in each chapter. They cover the terms included in CCEA's GCSE Religious Studies glossary.

LEARNING OUTCOMES

At the end of each chapter there is a useful table to track learning. These tables are designed to check knowledge and understanding, and highlight any areas that need improvement.

GLOSSARY

Pages 78–80 provide a valuable glossary of key terms.

INDEX

Pages 82–83 provide a useful index of key words.

BIBLE TRANSLATION

For all Bible quotations and references, this book uses the Good News Bible.

CHAPTER 1

THE EXISTENCE OF GOD

The meaning of the terms theist, atheist and agnostic

THEIST

Theism is the belief that there is a God who is the creator and ruler of the universe and actively involved in the world. Theism can include **monotheism** (belief in one God) and **polytheism** (belief in more than one god). The only thing all theists have in common is that they believe that at least one god exists. A theist can follow any world religion or simply have their own thoughts about God.

> **KEY TERMS**
>
> **Theist:** A person who believes in the existence of God.
>
> **Monotheism:** The belief in one God.
>
> **Polytheism:** The belief in the existence of many gods. It is viewed by many as the opposite of monotheism.

ATHEIST

The word atheism comes from the Greek negative *a* which means 'without,' and *theos* which means 'god.' Atheism is the lack of belief in a god and/or the belief that there is no god. Atheists can be categorised into two groups:

- Strong atheists actively believe and state that no god exists. They argue against the existence of the Christian God or any other god. Strong atheists can be challenging in their conversations with theists and try to disprove theistic beliefs.

- Weak atheists simply exercise no faith in God. Some atheists maintain that there is a lack of evidence to affirm God's existence. Others argue that the idea of God's existence is illogical and contrary to the evidence at hand.

Although not all atheists hold the same views, there are some beliefs that many share:

- God, the devil and angels do not exist.
- There is no supernatural realm, including ghosts or spirits.
- Miracles cannot occur.
- Evolution is a scientific fact.

AGNOSTIC

The word agnostic comes from the Greek *agnostos*, which means 'unknowable'. **Thomas Henry Huxley**, a British biologist, first used the term 'agnostic' in 1869 to describe someone who believes certain things are unknowable, such as the existence of God. An agnostic is not simply a person who has not made up their mind about the existence of

God or who cannot decide one way or another. An agnostic thinks it impossible to know whether or not God exists, or at least impossible at the present time. An agnostic suspends judgement and remains uncertain, saying that there is not enough evidence to confirm or deny the existence of God, the afterlife, miracles or anything else supernatural.

HUMANIST

Humanism is a system of thought that does not rely on belief in any gods or the teaching of any religious books. Humanists think that the answers to questions, such as 'What is the purpose of life?' come from what human beings have investigated or figured out. Humanists are atheist or agnostic.

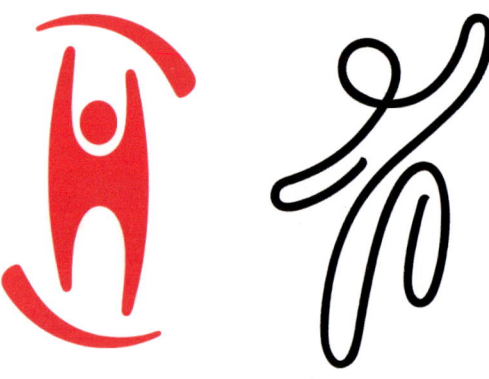

Some Humanist beliefs include:

- People don't have to follow a religion to be moral. Being good and not harming others is a principle based on human nature and human experience.
- There is no life after death. Humanists think people only have one life so they should do the best they can while they are alive. This means treating other people with respect to make the world a better place for everyone.
- Society should be secular (non-religious). However, there should be religious toleration, with people free to practice their religion as long as it does not persecute or harm others.
- It is very important to maintain a sustainable environment for future generations and to show responsibility towards the other creatures on the planet.

KEY TERMS

Agnostic: A person who is uncertain if God exists or not because there is insufficient evidence.

Atheist: A person who believes that there are convincing reasons and arguments to conclude that God does not exist.

Humanist: A person who believes that human experience and rational thinking, rather than religious teachings, provide a moral code to live by.

IN A GROUP

Read the following statements and decide if the person is a theist, an atheist or agnostic.

"The man asked if I believed in God. 'No.' I replied 'I know him. It's different.'"
Jackie Pullinger (1944–), Christian missionary in Hong Kong.

"It is wrong for a man to say that he is certain of the objective truth of any position."
TH Huxley (1825–1895), English scientist.

"We are all atheists about most of the gods that humanity has ever believed in. Some of us just go one god further."
Richard Dawkins (1941–), writer and broadcaster.

"Some scientists say that if the world were to stop revolving, we'd all disintegrate. But the world keeps on going. Something must be holding us all in place … but what it is I couldn't tell you."
Charlie Chaplin (1889–1997), performer and comedian.

"Humanists do not see that there is any obvious purpose to the universe, but that it is a natural phenomenon with no design behind it."
Stephen Fry (1957–), comedian, actor and broadcaster.

"I believe that there is a creator God: A God that created the universe and human life at the centre of it."
Delia Smith (1941–), cookery writer and television presenter.

Arguments for the existence of God

Can the existence of God ever be proved or disproved, one way or the other? Many people have concluded that it is unreasonable to believe in God because there is no evidence for his existence.

On the other hand, some people argue that there is evidence to suggest that God exists. These are known as theistic arguments. Traditionally, these arguments are associated with Christianity. There are four of these arguments to study in detail on your course.

KEY TERMS

Belief: This is something that people accept to be true or exists when they may not necessarily have proof.

Existence: The state or fact of existing. This term is frequently used when talking about God.

Theistic argument: A religious argument claiming there is evidence for the existence of God.

Reason: The power to determine truth by rational means.

PHILOSOPHERS AND THINKERS

St Thomas Aquinas (1225–1274) was an Italian Dominican monk, and a hugely influential philosopher, theologian and writer. His ideas still have influence in the Catholic Church today.

William Paley (1743–1805) was a Christian clergyman and philosopher who argued that the signs of design in the world justified belief in the existence of God.

Isaac Newton (1642–1727) was an English mathematician, physicist and theologian. He is most famous for his work on gravity and forces of motion.

David Hume (1711–1776) was a Scottish philosopher, historian and economist. He is especially known for his doubts about religious ideas and his agnostic views.

THE FIRST CAUSE ARGUMENT (also called the cosmological argument)

Everything that exists in the universe has been caused by something else. This means that the universe itself has been caused by someone or something. For theists, this is God.

The First Cause argument goes back to ancient Greek philosophy. It was developed by Arab scholars in the Middle Ages and used as an argument in Islam for the existence of God. The First Cause argument was first developed in a Christian context by **St Thomas Aquinas**. He was a Dominican monk who tried to use reason or logic to persuade people that God existed. Where did all the planets in the universe come from? What caused everything to happen? Aquinas argued that 'nothing comes from nothing'. Everything in the universe has been brought into being, or caused, by something else.

Aquinas argued that everything is part of a chain of cause and effect. Something causes something to happen, which causes something else to happen, and so on. When traced back, the universe must have had a first cause, that is, something that made it all happen in the first place and set it in motion. This first cause must be eternal otherwise it, too, would need something to make it to exist. Aquinas called this first cause the 'uncaused cause'. The uncaused cause is God. Aquinas concluded that because there is a universe, there has to be a God who made that universe. Therefore, God exists.

> The First Cause argument can be illustrated with a line of dominoes. A domino falls because another one knocks it over; it then causes another to fall, and so on. If you go back to the first domino, it did not fall over by itself; it had to be pushed by someone or something.

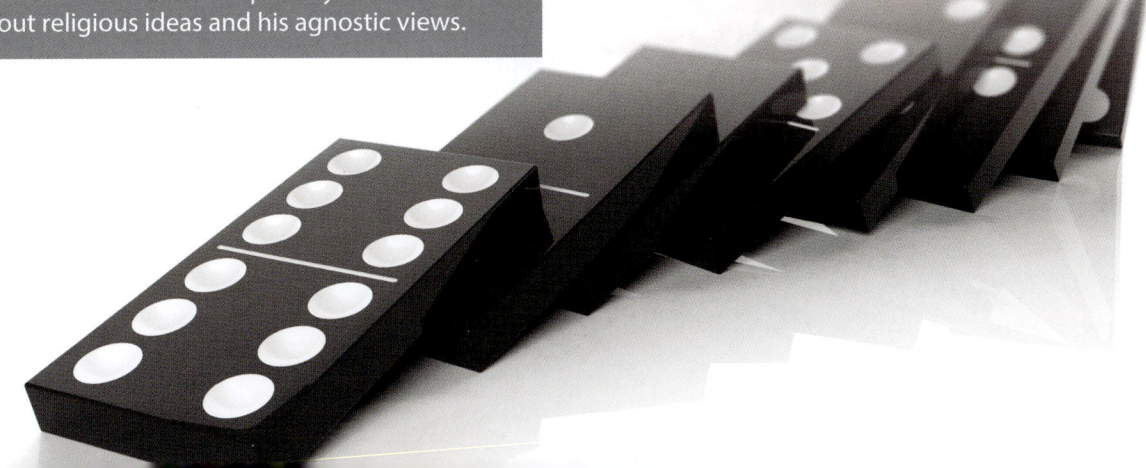

PHILOSOPHERS AND THINKERS

Richard Swinburne (1934–) is a Professor of Philosophy at the University of Oxford. For more than 50 years he has been influential in putting forward philosophical arguments for the existence of God.

Francis Bacon (1561–1626) was an English philosopher and a pioneer of modern scientific thought. He was also a very important political figure with influence in the royal court.

Bertrand Russell (1872–1970) was a British philosopher, mathematician, writer and social activist. He was born into an aristocratic family but described himself as a socialist. He was also a pacifist who actively campaigned against war and the use of nuclear weapons.

Sigmund Freud (1856–1939) was an Austrian doctor, who was the founder of psychoanalysis. This is a method of treating a troubled patient through dialogue. He was also considered an expert on the human mind and human behaviour.

KEY TERMS

First Cause argument: The theory that everything has a cause apart from God, who is the first cause, the 'uncaused'. This theory is used to argue in support of the existence of God. Also known as the cosmological argument.

Design argument: An argument that claims the existence of God can be inferred from the intricate design and complexity of the world in which people live. Also known as the teleological argument.

Religious experience: An experience that is caused by God rather than by ordinary or natural processes. Religious believers argue that a miracle is a type of religious experience. Also known as a spiritual experience.

Moral argument: An argument for the existence of God, based on the idea that all people have an instinctive sense of right and wrong that comes from God.

Strengths

This argument is a simple explanation, and many people would claim that a simple explanation is often the correct one. If this claim is to be believed, then it is logical to accept that God is the creator of the universe as it is the simplest explanation.

Scientific ideas, such as the Big Bang theory, can support the First Cause argument. If God is behind the Big Bang (see page 23), then God is the 'first cause' that brought the universe into existence.

Rejecting this argument requires something more complicated. Logic states that things exist because something or someone has brought them into existence. So, since the universe exists, it's only logical to assume that someone had caused it to exist. This being must have been someone who was omnipotent, eternal, and who is absolutely self-sufficient – qualities that can be attributed to God.

Weaknesses

Some people look at this argument for the existence of God and conclude that it can just as easily prove that God *does not exist*. If the first cause can be eternal, then why can the whole chain of cause and effect not be eternal? They argue there is no logical need for an uncaused cause. Perhaps the universe had no beginning, or perhaps it just started and there was nothing to cause it to start.

This argument raises the question 'Who or what caused God?' To say that God is eternal and has always been in existence is not sufficient to prove God's existence to atheists or agnostics.

Evidence to support or reject this argument

Aquinas never called his argument a 'proof' for the existence of God, but a way of reasoning which could lead to a conclusion. It is a route to follow to explore the world we live in. Aquinas was a Catholic monk, already convinced of the existence of God, and he was addressing this argument to believers like himself. The problem is that it is not believers who need this argument, only unbelievers, who may not feel it necessary to examine who started everything in the universe. The First Cause argument only really makes sense to theists who already believe in God.

THE ARGUMENT FROM DESIGN
(also called the teleological argument)

Looking at the world around us and seeing how beautiful and complex it is, proves it has been designed. This designer is God.

The argument from design is associated with

William Paley, a Christian philosopher. He argued that if people look at the universe around them, they will see that it has been very carefully designed. Think about the Earth in relation to the Sun. If the Earth was any closer or further away from the Sun it could not sustain life in all the variety people see around them. Many natural things have the appearance of being well thought out, for example, the design and order in a beehive or a snowflake. Why do all the things in nature seem to have the signs of being designed? Paley argued, "Design must have had a designer. That designer must have been a person. That person is God."

William Paley used the example of a traditional wind-up watch to explain his argument:

> "Imagine stumbling across a watch lying on the ground in an uninhabited place. You lift the watch and look at its intricate machinery of wheels and cogs. Do you think the watch was created by accident? You would be more inclined to think it was made by a skilled watchmaker. Yet the universe is far more intricate than a watch. Could it exist by chance? Does it require a designer? The implications are obvious. Something as complicated as the universe demands a designer who has put it together."

To support his idea, Paley referred to the construction of a human eye. Like the watch in his analogy, a human eye is a complex mechanism and to Paley it was obvious that the various parts of the eye had not come about by random chance. The efficient and well-designed structure are the work of a designer – God.

Strengths

The use of the watchmaker analogy in this argument makes it simple and straightforward to follow: it moves from something within human experience (a watch) to try to explain something beyond it (the creation of the universe). The argument is not necessarily incompatible with evolution and the Big Bang theory, as both of these processes could be part of the design of the universe. The concept of God as designer reinforces the idea that God is involved in the history of the universe and is therefore omnipotent, omniscient and omnibenevolent. The design argument gives a purpose to the universe, rather than having blind nature moving in a random direction. This in turn gives the universe meaning.

There are other examples to suggest design in the world around us, for example:

- DNA molecules, which contain all the information necessary to build a new creature, are so complex that many argue that they could not have arisen by chance alone.

- Scientist **Isaac Newton** used the thumbprint as evidence of the existence of God. Each person has an individual and unique thumbprint, even if they are identical twins. Newton argued that this pointed to a designer rather than random chance.

Weaknesses

Many people argue that the universe doesn't always seem so well-designed. There are major problems, such as earthquakes, volcanoes, floods and tsunamis, implying that there is no designer and that the Earth is simply the result of random chance. Darwin's theory of evolution (see page 21) presented a serious challenge to the argument from design, by saying that living things were not designed but have adapted to the world in order to survive.

Philosopher **David Hume** argued that there were big flaws in any argument for God based on design in the universe. Hume wrote his ideas in secret, as they challenged Christian teaching about God (a crime in the eighteenth century). They were published after he died. Hume's ideas have influenced a lot of people, particularly atheists and agnostics. Hume argued there were 'hidden assumptions' in the design argument, for example:

- Just because the design of the universe is complicated doesn't mean that there was just one designer who was responsible. The design argument might prove there are many gods; it does not prove there is one God.
- Even if we agree that God designed the universe, how do we know that God is still there? He might have designed the universe and gone off somewhere else to create something better.

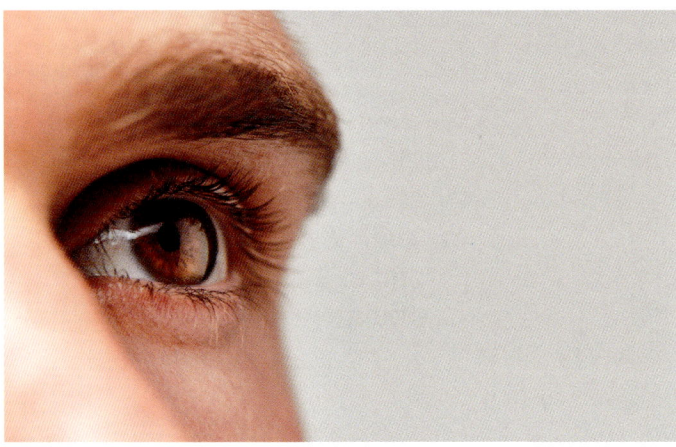

- Pointing out examples of good design, like the human eye, does not necessarily mean that a good God designed these things. The world is often faulty and imperfect, so perhaps God is cruel and not good at all.

Evidence to support or reject this argument

Many people can find evidence for design in nature by observing the world around them. However, there have been some serious challenges from science, including the theory of evolution. Also, while the universe may seem well-designed, but there is much that could be called bad design, such as natural disasters and disease. This could lead to people questioning the wisdom and goodness of the designer.

In the late twentieth century, some philosophers thought this argument was worth reviving, calling it 'intelligent design'. This is the idea that all creatures were created more or less in their present forms by an intelligent designer. Supporters of this argument claim that some biological features are too complex to be the result of evolution.

QUESTIONS

1. (i) Name the argument for the existence of God associated with St Thomas Aquinas. [1]
   (ii) What object did William Paley use in his argument for the existence of God? [1]
   (iii) What is polytheism? [1]
   (iv) What is monotheism? [1]
   (v) Name one religion that is monotheistic. [1]

2. Explain the difference between a theist and an agnostic. [5]

3. Do you think there is evidence to support the idea of an intelligent designer? Give reasons for your answer. [5]

4. "God is not at work in the world today." Do you agree or disagree? Give reasons for your answer. [5]

THE ARGUMENT FROM RELIGIOUS EXPERIENCE

Some people argue that God can be experienced. This may be through incidents such as:

- Answered prayer.
- A miracle being performed.
- God speaking in a dream or vision.
- Feeling God's presence while worshipping.

Because some people have experienced these things, they argue that God must exist. If people experience something, is that enough evidence to say that it is real? Most of the time, the evidence of their senses is good enough for people to trust that what they see or feel is real. In everyday situations, they do not usually doubt the evidence of their senses. The argument from religious experience takes the same approach. If people feel the presence of God, or see an angel, or hear a heavenly voice, such an experience is good enough, says the argument. After the experience, they should be able to say 'I have proof that there is a God, because I have had a religious experience.'

Some religious believers would say that having a religious experience can go beyond the five senses people use every day. In a special moment, God may make it possible for someone to see an angel or hear a heavenly voice, while no one else can see or hear anything. In moments like these, God has chosen to reveal something to a particular person. Sometimes a religious experience can bring a dramatic change in a person's life. This is often used as further evidence that that experience is 'real' rather than an imaginary one.

Strengths

Many people are more likely to believe something if it has been experienced, so human experience of God is the best evidence available that God exists. There are countless numbers of people throughout the world claiming to have had a religious experience. For many, the sheer amount of testimony is proof that God is responsible for the experience and therefore probably exists. These people include leaders from some of the world's religions as well as 'ordinary' people today.

Philosopher **Richard Swinburne** sets out what he calls the 'principle of credulity'. If a person believes God was present people should accept what a person experiences unless they can prove otherwise. People usually tell the truth. Swinburne considered that the argument from religious experience, when combined with the First Cause argument and the argument from design, made a very strong case for theism.

Weaknesses

A religious experience is usually something very private or personal for a believer. This means they can be open to doubt. Some people would argue that there is very little evidence to show someone has had a religious experience, as the so-called experience could be the result of someone's imagination and nothing to do with God. Another problem is that if God exists, and gives people religious experiences, then why do some people get to experience him and not everyone? Surely this is not fair.

Francis Bacon pioneered the scientific method. Considered a genius by some, his ideas are important when considering whether or not a religious experience could be valid. Bacon said that, although it is important to rely on our senses, we must find ways of making sure they do not deceive us. In establishing reliable evidence, Bacon would have said that a one-off individual experience is not good enough. You need to have seen something several times and there needs to be more than one witness. For many people an important consideration is whether or not a religious experience can satisfy these criteria.

The Religious Experience Research Centre

The Religious Experience Research Centre was founded by Sir Alister Hardy in 1969 in Oxford. Hardy asked the general public to send him descriptions of their own religious experiences. Over the years, the centre has built up an archive with over six thousand accounts of first-hand religious or spiritual experiences. These testimonies come from people across the world. The RERC currently has a group of researchers working on a range of projects. They organise seminars and conferences, and publish an online journal.

Evidence to support or reject this argument

One of the main objections to religious experiences is that a dream or vision can be interpreted in different ways. Philosopher **Bertrand Russell** made this point when he stated, "We can make no distinction between the man who eats little and sees heaven, and the man who drinks too much and sees snakes." This does not mean that someone is deliberately lying, but it does not make their experience real either. Psychologist **Sigmund Freud** believed that religious experience was an illusion that came from feelings of frustration in the course of a person's upbringing. Many people would say that religious experiences lack proof. Therefore, so does this argument.

However, just because religious experiences can be difficult to prove does not mean that they are not real. There is evidence to suggest that many people have religious experiences. Surely, believers argue, they cannot all be mistaken?

Examples of religious experience

Moses and the burning bush

Moses had fled from Egypt and was living in the land of Midian. One day he was out looking after sheep and goats when he came to Sinai, the holy mountain. He saw a strange sight. There was a bush that seemed to be on fire, but it was not being burnt up. Moses was puzzled and started to go closer. God spoke to Moses from the bush, telling him not to come any closer and to take off his sandals as he was on holy ground. God told Moses that he had seen how cruelly his people were being treated in Egypt. He intended to rescue them and bring them to a good land where they could live. God revealed to Moses that he had a plan for him – he was to go back to Egypt and tell Pharaoh that the Israelite slaves had to be set free. God reassured Moses that he would be with him as he carried out this task.

Muhammad has a vision of the Angel Jibril

Muhammad is the prophet of Islam. He was born in Mecca in the sixth century AD. Muhammad did various jobs, and finally became a trader, travelling with camels across the desert. In the early years of Muhammad's life, Mecca had a reputation for being a centre for idol worship. Muhammad instinctively knew that this was wrong, and he would often go alone into the hills outside Mecca to pray to God. On one of these occasions, Muhammad had the experience that was to change his life. He was praying in a cave when the Angel Jibril appeared to him and said he was to be God's prophet and teach people the ways of Islam. The angel told Muhammad to recite some verses. These were the first verses of the Qur'an, the holy book of Islam. Over several years, the whole Qur'an was revealed to Muhammad. Muslims regard him as being the last and final of God's prophets.

ACTIVITY

Use the Internet to research other examples of religious experience from different world religions.

For example:
- The Buddha's enlightenment (Buddhism).
- Guru Nanak's experience in the River Bein (Sikhism).
- Saul on the road to Damascus (Christianity).

PHILOSOPHERS AND THINKERS

Immanuel Kant (1724–1804) was a German philosopher whose writings and ideas had a significant impact on metaphysics, ethics and the theory of knowledge.

Cardinal John Newman (1801–1890) was a theologian and philosopher, who became a cardinal in the Catholic Church after converting from the Church of England at the age of 44.

Edward Osborne Wilson (1929–) is an American zoologist who is an expert in the social behaviour of all animals, including humans. Much of his research has involved the study of ants, on which he is also a leading authority.

THE MORAL ARGUMENT

People know the difference between right and wrong. For the moral argument, this in-built moral law is evidence of God.

The moral argument claims that most people are aware of their moral duties and responsibilities. Sometimes people make bad choices and act in the wrong way, but they usually realise this was not the right way to behave. From birth, humans are programmed with an in-built moral law. This suggests to some people that there is a being who is the source of this moral law. Moral values and duties exist; therefore God exists.

Philosopher **Immanuel Kant** was one of the first philosophers to develop the moral argument. He dismissed the First Cause argument and the argument from design as being invalid. Kant thought that with our limited human knowledge, it was impossible for us to discover an infinite God, far beyond human understanding. However, he argued that God could be found in a practical way through the feelings people have about how to behave. For example: 'I ought to help out; it's not right to leave all the work to one person' or 'If I want to pass my exams, I must get down to some revision'. Kant argued that everyone feels a sense of obligation to do the right thing. It is not something that people invent for themselves but comes from an outside source, God.

Why do we have a guilty conscience if we do something wrong? **Cardinal John Newman** argued that a guilty conscience is God's voice inside our head. As God has programmed us to know right from wrong, whenever we do something wrong our conscience switches on, reminding us of what we should have done, by making us feel ashamed.

Strengths

This argument appeals to a common sense of right and wrong. Some moral decisions might be controversial, but there are many moral questions where most people would agree. For example, it is wrong to steal or commit murder. It is common for a person to feel a sense of injustice if they are being mistreated and people tend to feel good about themselves if they perform a kind action.

The moral argument is consistent with beliefs about God in Christianity, Judaism and Islam. God is the ultimate source of goodness and expects certain standards of behaviour, communicated to people through laws and commands. A religious believer will naturally want to trace the origin of their moral values to God.

Weaknesses

For some people, establishing that there are common ideas of right and wrong does not prove the existence of God. There are other explanations that are just as valid.

American zoologist **Edward Osborne Wilson** argues that moral knowledge does not come from God but from how people have evolved. Wilson argues that, as a species, humans have learnt that they have a much better chance of surviving through co-operation, helping each other out and avoiding killing and stealing from each other. So, our moral knowledge is no great mystery. If humans had not learnt that it pays to be sociable, we would either be a solitary animal or extinct.

Psychologist **Sigmund Freud** explained morality, and in particular feelings of guilt, in psychological terms. A guilty conscience is not the voice of God, but a sense of morality that has come from a person's upbringing, mainly through their parents. There is no need for belief in God.

Evidence to support or reject this argument

Morality can be explained without the need for God, so there is no need to bring God into the argument at all. Surely the understanding of psychology and evolution of morality is enough to explain why people have a sense of right and wrong. This can be supported by observing that atheists and agnostics can act in a responsible and moral way, without the need for a moral governor. Immanuel Kant believed that everyone had a sense of moral duty, but he did not argue that this was definite proof of the existence of God. The moral argument is only valid if there is an absolute moral law that must be followed by all people everywhere. Many people today believe morality is all about making the right choice depending on the situation, so being morally good can depend on an individual's own code of conduct. It could also be argued that some people seem to have no sense of morality and commit dreadful crimes, such as genocide and torture.

However, some religious believers would argue that faith in God motivates many people to do good works, selflessly putting others before themselves. Would they really do this, putting themselves through suffering and hardship, because of evolution or upbringing as a child?

SUMMARY

Can philosophical arguments prove that God exists? How effective are these arguments in trying to persuade a non-believer that God exists? It is probably true that very few people have a religious faith because they have been convinced by a philosophical argument. However, many of the ideas in these theistic arguments can help to support and develop a religious faith.

Some arguments a theist might give for believing in God:

- Many people would say that without belief in God, life would have no meaning or purpose. The universe could not just have started by itself and everything seems to be carefully designed. For other people, the beauty of nature makes them aware of the presence of God. For some, a personal experience of God may have convinced them that God exists. An example is Nicky Cruz, the New York ex-gang member who experienced a religious conversion and became a Christian.
- Another reason is that people have a sense of right and wrong, so there must be a God who gives it to them. A guilty conscience is God's voice telling people that they have done wrong.

IN A GROUP

What are the reasons for supporting or rejecting each argument? Share your views with three or four others in your class. Which argument, if any, would you choose as being the most convincing?

You could record your discussion on a chart like the one below:

ARGUMENT	STRENGTHS	WEAKNESSES	OVERALL CONCLUSION
First Cause argument			

- Many people claim that belief in God brings a spiritual peace or satisfaction, which cannot be found anywhere else. For some people, belief in God brings them comfort in difficult circumstances.
- A child growing up in a religious family may accept that God exists because this is what they have been taught from an early age. They may not be able to say why they believe in God, only that he does exist. Some people would say this is 'blind faith' and does not show the existence of God at all. However, others might argue that the reason the family believes and has passed on their faith is because it is true and this is God at work.

Some arguments an atheist might give for not believing in God:

- There is a lack of any real evidence that God exists. The traditional arguments for God's existence are not convincing. There is no evidence that miracles happen or that there is a God who answers prayer.
- Today there are scientific explanations for most things, including the origin of the universe. In the past, people accepted the explanations put forward in holy books as they had no other way of understanding the world they lived in. Belief in God belongs to a pre-scientific era when there were many things in the universe that could not be explained.
- There are too many examples of meaningless suffering in the world. If God exists, then why doesn't he stop evil and prevent natural disasters? Sometimes a person experiences a personal tragedy which leads them to doubt the existence of a loving and powerful God.
- Many people seem to be able to live happy and fulfilled lives without the need to believe in God.

IN A GROUP

Organise a debate with the motion:

"Belief in God is not something you can prove. It is something that you know."

Working in groups of three or four:

- Decide whether your group is for or against the motion.
- Prepare a speech for or against the motion and select a speaker to represent your group to the class.
- Start the debate. Your teacher will select a chairperson to keep order.

 ## QUESTIONS

1. Describe an example of a religious experience you have studied. [5]
2. Outline how the moral argument supports the existence of God. [5]
3. Explain how religious experience can provide evidence for the existence of God. [5]
4. Do you think it is important for religious believers to provide evidence for the existence of God? Give reasons for your answer. [5]
5. "It is foolish to deny the existence of God." Do you agree with this statement? Give reasons for your answer. [5]
6. "All arguments for the existence of God are unconvincing." Do you agree or disagree? Give reasons for your answer showing that you have considered different points of view. [10]

The debate between creationism and science about the origin of the universe

> **KEY TERMS**
>
> **Creationism:** The belief that God created the world as outlined in a sacred text such as the book of Genesis in the Bible. It is sometimes interpreted to denote rejection of evolution.
>
> **Genesis:** The first book of the Bible, which includes the Jewish and Christian creation story of God being the one who made the world we live in.

CREATION IN JUDAISM AND CHRISTIANITY

According to the book of Genesis, the first book in the Bible, God created the universe in six days, and then rested on the seventh, as outlined in the diagram below. This account of creation is shared by both Christians and Jews.

How people relate to the universe

In the Genesis account of creation, God gave human beings an important role – they have to look after what he has created. This means people must act as stewards or guardians. Humans can use the Earth's resources, but in a responsible way, not taking the Earth for granted or spoiling God's creation. For example, animals can be eaten as food, but not hunted to extinction. The world is not owned by humans but 'on loan' from God. Christians believe that one day we will be held accountable for the way we have looked after the world.

The place of humanity in the created order

The account in Genesis shows that God planned the creation of the world and made it for humans to live in. Everything happens in logical steps, leading up to a climax – the creation of humankind. People are not created along with all the other mammals but are different. Only humans are made in the image of God, no other species. This suggests that humans are capable of having a special relationship with God. Being made in the image of God could also mean that humans share something of the nature of God.

DAY 1: In the beginning, the Earth had no form and everything was in total darkness. God created light and separated light from darkness. He called the light 'Day' and the darkness 'night'.

DAY 2: God created a dome over the earth which he called 'sky'.

DAY 3: God commanded all the water below the sky to come together in one place, so that the land would appear. He called the water 'sea' and the land 'earth'. The dry land produced vegetation.

DAY 4: God commanded lights to appear in the sky to separate day from night. He created two larger lights: the Sun to rule over the day and the Moon to rule over the night. God also created stars.

DAY 5: God created all kinds of creatures that live in the water and all kinds of birds.

DAY 6: God created animals to live on the Earth, domestic and wild, large and small. Finally, he created humans in his own image. God blessed them and gave them the responsibility of looking after everything he had made. When God had finished creating everything, he looked at what he had made and was pleased with it.

DAY 7: Creation was finished and God rested. God blessed the seventh day and set it apart as special.

FURTHER THINKING

For religious believers who accept the Genesis account of creation, how might this belief affect their views on:

- Animal rights
- Conservation

Share your views with a partner.

KEY TERMS

Brahma: The Hindu god in control of creating.

Brahman: Many Hindus believe Brahman is the one supreme God, seen in many different forms.

Shiva: The Hindu god in control of destroying what needs to be replaced.

Vishnu: The Hindu god in control of preserving and sustaining everything.

CREATION IN HINDUISM

Hindus have many different versions of how the universe was created. They believe that Brahman is the source of all life. There are thousands of different gods and goddesses in Hinduism, who are all aspects of Brahman. The three most important gods in Hinduism are Brahma (The Creator), Vishnu (The Preserver) and Shiva (The Destroyer). Hindus believe that creation is a constant cycle. The universe is constantly being re-created and destroyed.

In some Hindu traditions, everything was created out of a part of Brahma's body – head, hands, body, legs, etc. Everything is therefore part of Brahma.

The Rig Vedas are among the oldest Hindu texts. They contain the story of a cosmic egg from which all the creatures emerged. Brahma, the creator god, is often pictured coming out first.

Some Hindu scriptures suggest that creation does not have a definite starting point. It came out of Brahman and is more like a wave. The water rises into a crest before falling into a trough and so the process goes on and on. Most Hindus today are perfectly happy to accept scientific theories about how the universe came into being, as long as room is left for the universal force behind the universe, which is Brahman.

A Hindu creation story

Before this time began, there was no heaven and no Earth. A huge, dark, ocean washed upon the shores of nothingness. A giant cobra floated on the waters, with Vishnu lying asleep within its coils (as shown in the diagram below). Everything was so peaceful and silent that Vishnu slept undisturbed. A humming noise that sounded like 'OM' began to grow and filled the emptiness. The night had ended, and Vishnu awoke. As the dawn began to break, from Vishnu's navel grew a magnificent lotus flower. In the middle of the blossom sat Brahma. Vishnu then commanded Brahma to create the world. A wind swept up the waters and Vishnu and the serpent vanished.

Brahma remained in the lotus flower. He raised his arms and commanded the wind and the ocean to be calm. Then Brahma split the lotus flower into three. He stretched one part into the heavens. He made another part into the Earth and with the third part of the flower he created the skies. The Earth was bare, and so Brahma set to work. He created all kinds of plants and vegetation. Next, he created the animals and all the other creatures to live on the land. He made birds to fly in the air and fish to swim in the sea. The world was soon full of life and the air was filled with the sounds of Brahma's creation.

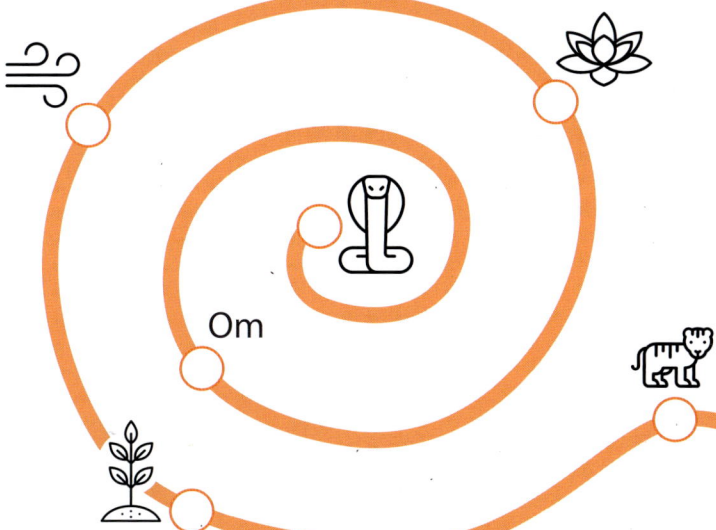

How people relate to the universe

In Hindu belief, the universe is God's body. Everything in the universe, including humans, are a part of this body and are therefore sacred. So to harm another person, an animal or a plant is to harm God's body of which everyone is a part. Hindus believe in the idea of *ahimsa*, the principle of non-violence. This means showing respect for all life forms, human, animal and vegetable. Another important idea in Hinduism is *karma*, the belief that all actions bring consequences. Belief in *karma* should encourage Hindus to take responsibility for their actions, including how they treat the rest of creation.

The place of humanity in the created order

For Hindus, time is not seen as a straight line, but a series of cycles that go on forever. This reflects the cycle of birth, death and re-birth that is part of human existence. Hindus believe in reincarnation. Human beings are born, grow old and die, and then their soul (the *atman*) is then re-born into another living being – human, animal or plant. Within Hindu tradition, humans are no more or less important than any other aspect of creation. Everything is ultimately a part of Brahman and everything will return to Brahman.

SCIENTIFIC IDEAS ABOUT THE ORIGINS OF THE UNIVERSE

The sacred texts of many of the world's religions are thousands of years old and were written before the age of science. As new discoveries were made, some of the traditional religious ideas were challenged.

PHILOSOPHERS AND THINKERS

Nicholaus Copernicus (1473–1543) was a Polish mathematician and astronomer. He discovered that all the planets were in orbit around the Sun, rather than the Earth being in the centre of the universe.

William Smith (1769–1839) was an amateur geologist known as 'The father of English geology'. He was especially interested in stratigraphy, a branch of geology that looks at the position and age of rock layers.

Charles Lyell (1797–1875) was a Scottish lawyer and geologist. He wrote a book suggesting the Earth's geological features took millions of years to form. Charles Darwin read this book during his time on the HMS *Beagle*.

Charles Darwin (1809–1882) was an English naturalist who studied biology. He is one of the main scientists who developed the theory of evolution.

The challenge of science

A great change in thinking took place in the sixteenth century and is associated with the name **Nicholaus Copernicus**. He was a Christian priest and also an astronomer. Until his time, people thought the Earth was the centre of the universe, with the Sun, Moon and stars revolving around it. This idea seemed to fit in with the creation account in Genesis. Copernicus stated that the Earth was just one of several planets orbiting the Sun in the solar system.

In the eighteenth and nineteenth centuries, scientists started to come up with other ideas that challenged the biblical view of creation:

William Smith was an amateur geologist with an interest in fossils. He noted that the deeper layers of rock were older than the ones nearer the surface, and that the fossils found in these layers were not like the ones he could see nearer the surface. He was one of the first to challenge the idea that creation happened in six days (that is, six periods of 24 hours) and suggested that God may have created different plants and animals at different stages in the history of the world.

Charles Lyell went further and suggested that creation was a more gradual process. He claimed that natural processes like erosion and sedimentation had taken millions of years to form the mountains and valleys we can see in the world and that this could be proved through rock formations and fossils. These processes are still happening, and the world is gradually changing all the time. Lyell's ideas challenged the idea that the Earth was 6000 years old and created in six days.

Charles Darwin is famous for his 'theory of evolution'. Many people have taken this as the most serious challenge to the Bible account of creation.

THE THEORY OF EVOLUTION

> **KEY TERMS**
>
> **Evolution:** A scientific theory that claims that life developed from simple organisms through natural selection.
>
> **Natural selection:** The process through which living organisms adapt and change.
>
> **Theistic evolution:** The belief that God controls evolution, as he created a world that could change and develop.

> **The work of Charles Darwin**
>
> Darwin studied natural science at Cambridge university and had a keen interest in geology. He was also a Christian. On a five-year voyage around the world on the ship HMS *Beagle*, he had the opportunity to study plants, animals and fossils. Darwin spent some time on the Galapagos Islands in the Pacific Ocean, observing finches and tortoises. His work there convinced him that all forms of life have evolved over millions of years. Darwin continued to develop his ideas once he returned from his voyages. Finally, as a result of his world expedition, discussions with like-minded scientists and his knowledge of fossils, he developed the theory of evolution by natural selection. Darwin wrote his ideas in the book *On the Origin of Species*, which was published in 1859, 28 years after his voyage ended. It was not his intention to challenge religious beliefs with his book, but many people reacted with fury.

Charles Darwin's theory of evolution was arguably the most important scientific theory to emerge in the nineteenth century. Today, it is the generally accepted explanation for the origin of life on the planet. The line of reasoning is as follows:

- Darwin looked at fossils and noted similarities between ancient plants and animals, and the ones in the world around him. He concluded that one species must have developed out of another.
- Plants and animals generally produce more offspring than can ever survive. Those with the characteristics most suited to the environment are most likely to survive by finding food, avoiding predators and resisting disease. These survivors can then breed successfully and pass on their characteristics to the next generation. Species that cannot adapt to their environment are less likely to survive and reproduce. This process is known as 'survival of the fittest'. Darwin called it 'natural selection'.
- Evolution happens through natural selection, as species gradually change and adapt. Plants and animals were not created in the form we see them today, as this has been the result of a process taking millions of years.
- Some species, such as humans, have developed relatively fast and become very complex. Others have evolved relatively slowly, such as some species of fish. The weaker species that do not adapt at all become extinct. Sometimes a species will evolve into two distinct species, each with different characteristics to suit their environments.
- Evolution implies that all living things are related. This means that all animals, plants and

every other living being have evolved from one simple life form. Evolution has led to one species becoming several, and so on until there are many millions, as there are today.

Darwin applied his theory to human beings as well as plants and animals. He concluded that, as humans share some of their physical characteristics with apes, the two species must be related in some way. This last point upset many religious people and Darwin's theory remains controversial today.

> **Evidence for evolution**
>
> - Fossils – A fossil is the preserved remains of a dead organism from millions of years ago. Fossil remains are found in rocks, with the simplest organisms found in the oldest rocks and the more complex organisms in the newest rocks. This supports the idea that simple life forms have gradually evolved into more complex ones.
> - Extinction – This means there are no longer any living individuals of a species. Animals that cannot adapt to their environment may become extinct. This may be caused by climate change, new diseases, new predators, or a single catastrophic event, such as a meteorite hitting the Earth. Two well-known examples of extinctions are the dinosaurs and a large flightless bird called the dodo. It is thought that dinosaurs could not cope with climate change, while the dodo was the victim of a new predator, the humans who settled on the birds' uninhabited island.

Some problems with Darwin's theory

Darwin's theory of evolution attempts to explain how life on Earth began. However, it does not address the question of how the universe was formed in the first place. While Darwin collected much evidence to support parts of his theory, such as natural selection, there is no direct evidence to conclusively prove that humans have evolved from apes, rather than being a separate species. The fossil record remains incomplete and cannot currently prove a direct link between humans and apes.

How Darwin's theory challenges creation in the Bible

The theory of evolution challenges the religious teachings that God created the Earth and all the living things in the form they are today. The idea that living things must adapt to their environment to survive goes against the idea that God has provided a perfect world for his creations. There is also the difficulty of explaining why God would create a species but then allow it to become extinct.

Evolution also challenges the idea of God as designer, as found in the argument from design. With the theory of evolution, there is no need for a designer or creator of the universe, as everything has happened by chance as one species has developed into another.

The theory of evolution challenges the timescale suggested in the Bible. According to the Genesis account of creation, God created sea creatures and birds on the fifth day. Then he created land animals and humans on the sixth day. In Darwin's theory, this took millions of years, not the six days in the Bible account.

In Genesis, God made all the different animals, then showed them to the first man so that he could name them. Darwin's theory suggests that all these species had evolved over time from common ancestors. According to the Bible, humans are special as they are the only ones created in the 'image' of God. In Darwin's theory, humans are not special as they have evolved just like everything else. Evolution challenges the idea that humans were placed by God as stewards over creation because humans are a relatively recent development in the evolutionary chain.

Evolution and Christianity

There are many different responses among Christians to the theory of evolution. Some Christians hold a creationist viewpoint. This means they believe that the Genesis account is giving literal, scientific truth. The Bible is the Word of God, and everything written in it, word for word, is true. This means the world and humanity are much younger than science tells us – only a matter of a few thousand years. As these Christians believe the creation account in the Bible is literally true, this means scientific theories, such as evolution, must be wrong. Some would argue that so called 'evidence' that the Earth is old, such as fossils, have been placed there by God to confuse people who do not accept the truth of the Bible.

Some Christians accept Darwin's theory and believe that science and the Bible can both be right, but in different ways. Many Christians believe that the creation story in Genesis contains the truth that God is in control and created everything. However, they are prepared to accept that the six days of creation may not be six days as we know them. They might have been six periods of time, each period millions of years long. Some Christians argue that science explains how the world was created, while the Bible explains the role that God played in creation, so they have no difficulty accepting evolution. They regard the stories of creation in Genesis as myths, but believe that they still contain important ideas. Theistic evolution is the belief that God controls evolution. He created the universe then guided the process by which all life has evolved from a simple organism.

Evolution and Hinduism

Some Hindus are not in agreement with evolution for the following reasons:

- Vishnu, the god who preserves Brahma's creation, has a role in evolution rather than it being left to chance.
- The existence of the *atman* (soul) is a very important idea in Hinduism. Evolution does not explain where the *atman* has come from.
- Evolution contradicts Hindu creation stories, if they are taken literally.

However, many Hindus do not have a problem with the theory of evolution. Brahma creates life on Earth, and for these people evolution is one of the many ways that Vishnu preserves life. Vishnu the preserver is evident in evolution by the fact that life is strengthened and continues. Also, many Hindus do not interpret the stories in their scriptures as literal, scientific truth. Instead, they are important for passing on religious and spiritual truths.

ACTIVITY

Science vs Evolution

The Genesis account of creation suggests the following:

- God created the universe out of nothing.
- Creation took six days.
- The Earth was created in the form we see today.
- The timescale in the Bible suggests the Earth is around 6000 years old.
- Human beings are special, and the only creatures made in the image of God.

For each statement, explain one way in which science or geology presents a challenge to this idea.

THE BIG BANG THEORY

KEY TERMS

Big Bang theory: A scientific theory that seeks to provide an explanation for the origins of the universe by reference to an initial 'explosion.'

Galaxy: A cluster of billions of stars, held together by gravity.

Red-shift: The change in wavelength of light from a star or galaxy as it moves away from Earth.

In the 1920s, the Big Bang theory was suggested as a scientific explanation for the creation of the universe. It was first proposed by Alexander Friedman, a Russian mathematician, then developed by Georges-Henri Lemaitre, who was a Belgian physicist and also a Catholic priest.

Most scientists now accept the theory, which states that all the material that makes up the universe was once compressed into a tiny, super-dense mass. For reasons that are not fully understood, around 14 billion years ago this mass exploded with enormous heat and energy – a 'big bang' – and the universe began to rapidly expand. As the fireball cooled, atoms formed, followed by galaxies and stars and eventually planets. It is thought that the Earth was formed around 4.5 billion years ago, when gravity pulled together gas and dust swirling around the young Sun. The Earth gradually cooled, and once it had the right conditions for life, living things formed naturally from chemicals and began to evolve. The universe is still expanding today, meaning that galaxies continue to move away from each other at great speed.

In the 1930s the astronomer Edwin Hubble used a powerful telescope to make detailed observations of the movements of the galaxies. He discovered that wavelengths of light coming from almost all galaxies display a red-shift, showing that they are moving away from us and from each other. This led him to conclude that the universe was expanding from a single point, providing strong support for the Big Bang theory.

The Big Bang theory and Christianity

For some Christians, the Big Bang and the Genesis story cannot go together. They believe that the Bible's account of creation is literally true in every way and that the Earth is around 6000 years old, which does not fit with the Big Bang. They believe that the Big Bang theory does away with the need for a divine creator, as it suggests the world came into being through natural processes.

However, there are Christians who accept the Big Bang theory. They say that if God created the whole universe out of nothing, in a short space of time, it must have been a very dramatic event – such as a big bang. They argue that the Big Bang theory supports the Genesis account of creation. To them, God was behind the 'Big Bang', so there is scientific evidence that God created the universe.

The Big Bang theory and Hinduism

For many Hindus, the Big Bang theory does not present a challenge to their belief in creation. It is a scientific theory that can sit alongside their religious beliefs. It does not contradict Hindu teaching on the continual cycle of creation, preservation and destruction. The Big Bang theory does not mention the *atman* (soul) and so there is no attempt to challenge its eternal nature.

Is it a waste of time worrying about where the universe came from?

Some people argue that worrying about where the Earth came from or when it will all end is pointless. They think it would be far better focusing on current concerns, like climate change, poverty or human rights. Most religious texts say very little about the origins or the end of the universe, so we should not be too concerned about such matters, but trust in God. Others argue that thinking about where they came from, and why, can help people to understand their place in the universe. This can affect the way they choose to live their lives.

 **FURTHER THINKING**

Do you accept a scientific explanation for our existence, a religious explanation or a combination of both?

What reasons do you have for your view? Is there any evidence to support your view?

SCIENCE AND RELIGION

Religion is much older than science. Many holy books record stories to explain how the universe and human life began. Primitive people did not have a great understanding of the natural world, so there was a lot for religion to try to explain. As scientific knowledge increases, there is less and less need for religious explanations. A phrase first used in the nineteenth century was 'God of the gaps'. This is the idea that God (or religion) is used to explain the things that science has no answers for yet. However, the gaps filled by religion are growing smaller all the time. Could science eventually replace religion if there are no more gaps to fill?

Arguments to challenge this idea include the following:

- Science deals with facts and how they should be understood. To investigate these facts, we need to use our senses. Religion also claims to deal with facts or 'truths', but these are discovered spiritually. To understand life fully, perhaps we need both a scientific and a religious understanding. Some people would say that religion asks the 'why' questions, whereas science asks 'how' questions.
- Most of the world's religions claim that the world was created by God and is based on laws that he put in place. The task of science is to discover these laws and understand them. This is proved by the fact that many scientists are religious believers.

Scientific truth and religious truth

Scientists can only conclude that something is true if they can demonstrate it to be so by experiment; they have to be able to show that each time they conduct the experiment the same thing happens. When the same result is obtained from an experiment that is repeated over and over again, it is known as empirical evidence and is the basis of scientific truth. Religious truth deals with faith and belief. People may say that they 'know' God but they cannot prove it in a scientific way. This can make it very difficult to persuade people who are sceptical or do not believe themselves.

 **QUESTIONS**

1. (i) Name one scientific theory about the origin of the universe. [1]
   (ii) Name one scientist who has written on the subject of creation. [1]
   (iii) Name the creator of the universe in any religion you have studied. [1]
   (iv) What is meant by 'natural selection'? [1]
   (v) Name one geologist who challenged the Bible's account of creation. [1]
2. Outline how the universe was created in one world religion you have studied. [5]
3. Explain why some religious believers accept the theory of evolution. [5]
4. "One day, science will have the answer to everything." Do you agree with this statement? Give reasons for your answer. [5]
5. "It is a waste of time worrying about where the universe came from or where it is going." Do you agree with this statement? Give reasons for your answer. [5]
6. "The theory of evolution does not necessarily challenge belief in God." Do you agree or disagree? Give reasons for your answer showing that you have considered different points of view. [10]

An Introduction to Philosophy of Religion

LEARNING OUTCOMES

Learning outcome	Know & understand	Need to revise	Completed
The meaning of the terms theist, atheist and agnostic • Theist • Atheist • Agnostic			

Arguments for the existence of God
• The First Cause argument (or the cosmological argument)
  - Strengths
  - Weaknesses
  - Evidence to support or reject the argument
• The argument from design (or the teleological argument)
  - Strengths
  - Weaknesses
  - Evidence to support or reject the argument
• The argument from religious experience
  - Strengths
  - Weaknesses
  - Evidence to support or reject the argument
• The moral argument
  - Strengths
  - Weaknesses
  - Evidence to support or reject the argument			

The debate between creationism and science about the origin of the universe • Creation stories from two different world religions • The views of two different world religions on the relationship between humanity and the created order • The challenge of science • The theory of evolution • The Big Bang theory • Scientific truth and religious truth			

CHAPTER 2
THE NATURE OF GOD

Ways of understanding and describing God

For religious believers who accept that God exists, it is important to consider what attributes and characteristics he may possess. An important question is whether God is actively involved with his creation or distinct from the world.

KEY TERMS

Attribute: A quality or feature that is regarded as a characteristic or inherent part of someone or something.

Existence: The state or fact of existing. This term is frequently used when talking about God.

Immanent: The belief that God is involved and present in his creation.

Transcendence: Comes from the Latin prefix trans meaning beyond. The belief that God is beyond and not limited by the world that he created.

Omnipotent: All-powerful; it is a quality essential to the nature of God. There is nothing that is beyond God or impossible for him to do.

Omniscient: All-knowing; a quality essential to the nature of God.

Omnipresent: Present everywhere. It is an attribute of God.

Omnibenevolent: All-good; it is a quality essential to the nature of God. God is totally loving and the source of all goodness.

Knowable: The idea that believers can have a personal relationship with God, who is described as a father or friend.

Unknowable: The belief that God is beyond human understanding and humans can never hope to know and understand him completely.

The following terms are often used to describe God:

IMMANENCE

An immanent God is one who is involved in the universe he has made. God did not just start off the world and then go away. He is not some 'far-off' being; God is actively involved in people's lives.

Christians believe that the Holy Spirit is God actively at work in the world today, guiding and inspiring individuals and the Church. This is one of the main reasons why Christians pray. They believe that God hears prayers and is active in answering them. God is still active in the world, guiding and inspiring people, just as he did in the early Church.

Many religious believers claim to have experienced God in some way. Religious experiences can include visions, witnessing a miracle or communicating with God through prayer (see Chapter 4, 'Experiencing God', for more detail).

TRANSCENDENCE

A transcendent God is separate and distinct from the universe. He is not controlled by the laws of the universe, such as time. He is beyond human understanding.

People worship a transcendent God as being the all-powerful creator of the universe. The universe depends on God as it would not exist without him. Their needs and concerns are nothing compared to the vastness and power of God. Transcendence is the opposite of immanence – humans cannot have a personal relationship with a transcendent God as he is not personally involved in their lives.

OMNIPOTENT

Omnipotent means 'all-powerful'. An omnipotent God has the ability to do anything and this power is exercised effortlessly.

In the Old Testament, one of the Hebrew titles for God is *el Shaddai*, which means 'self-sufficient' or 'almighty'. This shows that God's power is unlimited.

In the Bible, God is shown as being omnipotent in creation. He has made everything out of nothing, simply by commanding things to happen. The ten plagues that were sent to Egypt, recorded in the book of Exodus in the Old Testament, show an omnipotent God acting to save his people and showing his power to a stubborn Pharaoh.

The Bible also shows that God is omnipotent in salvation. God has a plan to redeem sinful humanity, as shown throughout the Bible story. In the life of Jesus, God is shown as omnipotent in the resurrection: by raising Jesus from the dead, God shows that he is more powerful than sin and death.

OMNISCIENT

Omniscient means 'all-knowing'. An omniscient God has all the knowledge in the universe – past, present and future. At creation, God created the world and everything in it, including knowledge. God has complete knowledge of everything the future holds, for the whole of the universe and for every individual person.

Christians believe that God has a plan for everyone even before they are born. The Bible says that even the hairs on a person's head are numbered by God. The knowledge of God is also complete – he does not gradually learn new things as we do but knows everything at once.

OMNIPRESENT

An omnipresent God is present everywhere, all the time. He cannot be contained even by the largest space possible. He is not simply a layer surrounding the universe as we know it and he does not simply exist in a kind of infinite, unending space. God is present to all space. This does not mean that at least a little part of God is dispersed throughout the infinite reaches of space. Instead, God in his whole being is present at every point of our space. Humans cannot see God, but belief in his omnipresence confirms that God sees each person all the time.

OMNIBENEVOLENT

Omnibenevolent means 'all-good'. An omnibenevolent God is absolutely good and there is no action, motive or anything else about him that is not purely good.

The Bible gives many examples of God's goodness, including Jesus' teaching, when he asserted that no one is truly good except God Himself. This means that although human beings can do good things, only God is omnibenevolent, or wholly good.

To believe in a perfect being, it is necessary to accept that God can be omnibenevolent. If God were simply a good and powerful being, but not totally good, then there could be a being of potentially greater benevolence – and someone with greater goodness would be greater than God.

KNOWABLE

A knowable God is a personal one. In some religions, God is described in personal terms, as though he has human qualities, for example as a father or friend. In this way, believers are showing that they can have a close and personal relationship with God.

The ultimate example of a personal God is the Christian belief that Jesus is God in human form. God spent time on Earth as a human, experiencing human life with all its suffering. Christians believe that the way to know more about God and his purpose for humanity is through a personal relationship with Jesus.

The word **anthropomorphic** literally means 'human form'. Sometimes, anthropomorphic language is used to describe God, meaning God is described as having human characteristics. For example, describing God as a father, shepherd, king or judge. The Bible refers to 'The right hand of God' as though God has limbs like a human being.

ACTIVITY

The spider diagram below gives some of the key terms used to describe God. Can you think of any other ways to describe God?

UNKNOWABLE

An unknowable God, by contrast, is beyond the limits of human understanding. Through reading scared texts and taking part in worship, believers can get to know something about the nature of God. However, humans can never hope to understand God completely. There is an overlap here with the idea of God's transcendence, where it is impossible to ever know God completely as he is beyond human understanding. This is the idea of an impersonal God.

In the Bible, God is described as being 'holy'. This Hebrew word means 'separate' or 'set apart'. The concept of 'holy' is so different from human experience, that it should provoke feelings of awe and respect, even fear. In Moses' encounter with God at the burning bush, he was told "Do not come any closer. Take off your sandals, because you are standing on holy ground." Moses then covered his face "because he was afraid to look at God" (Exodus 3:5 and 6). The holiness of God reinforces the idea of God as unknowable.

 **IN A GROUP**

The Ancient of Days (William Blake)

Sistine Chapel ceiling (Michaelangelo)

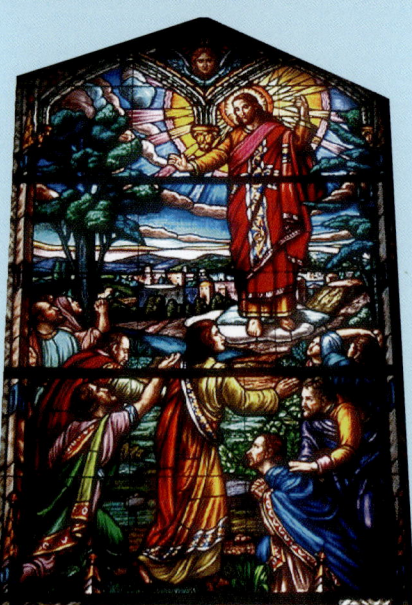
The Ascension of Christ (stained glass)

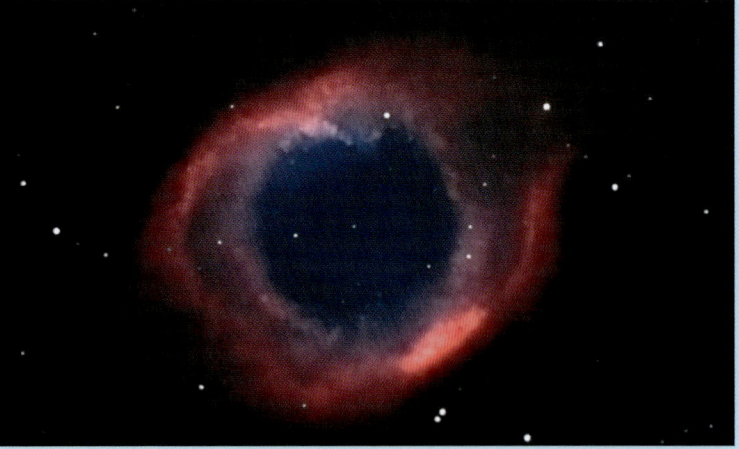
The Nelix Nebula

- Working in a group, look at the pictures and discuss what impression each gives of God. Make a list of the possible words that could be used to describe God.
- What do you think each of the artists is trying to show about the nature of God?

> **KEY TERMS**
>
> **Monotheism:** The belief in one God.
>
> **Polytheism:** The belief in the existence of many gods. It is viewed by many as the opposite of monotheism

MONOTHEISM

This is the belief in a single, all-powerful God, as opposed to believing in many gods. For example, Christianity, Islam and Judaism are monotheistic religions. In the Bible there is the command "Israel, remember this! The LORD—and the LORD alone—is our God." (Deuteronomy 6:4). The Qur'an states "Your God is one God; there is no God but He, the All-merciful, the All-compassionate" (Surah 2:163).

Monotheistic religions have certain features in common, arising from the belief in one God. This singular God is seen as being omnipotent and the creator of the universe. He is eternal and relies on no one else for his existence. God continues to act in the world and will one day judge the whole of humanity. Monotheistic religions often have an absolute approach to morality and decision making. This means there are set rules that must always be followed by all people. The commandment to do these things has come from the one true God.

POLYTHEISM

This is the belief in, or worship of, more than one god. Polytheism is part of the beliefs of Confucianism, Taoism and Shintoism in the east, and also contemporary tribal religions in Africa and the Americas. Some Hindus see their religion as polytheistic, though others believe that all the different gods are just part of Brahman. Polytheistic religions are widely practiced throughout the world and remain popular in their ancestral areas.

Some polytheistic beliefs are also popular in Western civilisation today, perhaps because more people are becoming interested in religions from the east. Unlike Christian, Jewish and Islamic teaching, there is often no absolute right and wrong associated with polytheism. Different cultures have their own ideas and each believer is free to worship the god(s) of his or her choice in the way that they choose. As a result, each person is free to behave as he or she sees fit. Although polytheism provides flexibility, critics say that it can leave some followers with no sense of ultimate purpose in life.

> **ACTIVITY**
>
> Design a series of revision flash cards to help you remember the key terms about the nature of God. You could use your resource to test your friends.

SOME QUESTIONS TO CONSIDER

1. Is it possible to truly know and understand God?

Most religious believers would agree that the omnipotent and transcendent creator of the universe could never be fully known or understood by human beings. However, they would also believe that God has given ways for people to understand something about him, if they choose to. Christians believe that we can know what God is like through Jesus. God came into the world to show people how much he loves them and that he cares enough to want to teach them things. Hindus might say that people cannot understand God all at once, because Brahman is too big an idea for the human mind, and that having different gods is a way of understanding Brahman a little better.

2. Can God be knowable and unknowable at the same time?

It might seem as if some of these ways of describing God contradict each other. How can religious believers think of God as both knowable and unknowable, immanent and transcendent? Here are some examples to show how God can be thought of in both ways:

- **Christianity** – The Trinity (see page 33) helps Christians to think of God as being both transcendent and immanent. God the Father is the transcendent creator of the universe. God the Son took human form in the person of Jesus – an immanent God. Christians believe God is active (immanent) in the world through the work of the Holy Spirit.
- **Hinduism** – Brahman is transcendent. However, Hindus believe that they can understand something of what Brahman is like through the many different gods and goddesses of Hinduism, which are knowable. They are all different aspects of Brahman's character and personality. Hindus pray and meditate as part of their worship and some say this had led them to have a personal experience of God.
- **Islam** – The Qur'an teaches that God is transcendent, "Say He is Allah the One … there is none like Him" (Surah 112). At the same time, however, Muslims pray five times a day believing that Allah hears and answers their prayers (immanence) because Allah is active in the world.

3. Is it disrespectful to use personal language to describe God?

An advantage of thinking of God as being personal is that he is close at hand. People can have a real relationship with him, as he is interested in their problems and hears their prayers. It can be comforting to think of God as a father or friend. On the other hand, some people think that care and discretion is needed when describing and addressing God. It is important not to be disrespectful or reduce God to the level of a human being. God is the creator of the universe and is beyond human understanding. Therefore, they say, he should not be described in human terms.

Another argument is that all human language about God is inappropriate and inadequate, as God is so far beyond human comprehension. Others argue that, if using personal language to describe God is helpful and comforting to believers, then there is nothing wrong with using it.

4. Is it wrong to make statues or images of God?

For Hindus worshipping at a shrine, images of one of the various gods are an important aid to worship. Hindus would say that they do not worship the statues, rather that the statues are there as a focus for worship. In some Christian traditions, for example, the Catholic Church, statues and pictures can also serve as an aid to worship.

However, both Islam and Judaism condemn the making of images for worship. This rule is set out in the Ten Commandments. Muhammad forbade the making of all images and removed all the idols from the Kaaba (a shrine in the city of Mecca, considered by Muslims to be the most sacred place on Earth). Some believers argue that as God has created everything in the world, nothing we make could ever be good enough, so making images of God reduces him to the level of human imagination.

IN A GROUP

What do you think about each of the questions above? What are the arguments for and against each suggestion?

QUESTIONS

1. (i) What is meant by the term omnipotent? [1]
   (ii) What is meant by the term omnipresent? [1]
   (iii) What word means that God is all-knowing? [1]
   (iv) Give one example of using personal language to describe God. [1]
   (v) Give one example of a religion that is monotheistic. [1]

2. Explain, giving examples, why some religious believers think of God as both transcendent and immanent. [5]

3. "It is wrong to use personal language to describe God, such as Father, friend." Do you agree with this statement? Give reasons for your answer. [5]

4. "God has no involvement in people's lives today." Do you agree or disagree? Give reasons for your answer showing that you have considered different points of view. [10]

Contrasting beliefs about the nature of God

THE CHRISTIAN UNDERSTANDING OF GOD – THE TRINITY

Christianity is a monotheistic religion, teaching that there is only one God. Christians also believe that God is not like any other being, which makes it difficult to describe God. One word that Christians use to describe God is 'holy', which means 'separate' or 'set apart'.

Christians believe that this one God exists in three persons. This is called the Trinity:

1. **God the Father** – God created the universe and answers prayers. For example, "Our father in Heaven…" This image of the father suggests that God loves human beings. As well as being the creator, God is the sustainer of everything and cares for all his creation. God the Father also acts as a judge and will punish people if they do wrong. However, God is also loving and will forgive anyone who shows they are sorry.

2. **God the Son** – This is God in the form of a man, Jesus, who lived on Earth. Jesus was born of a human mother and lived a human life but was sinless. Jesus showed people how to live in the right way and how to enter God's kingdom. The climax of his ministry of teaching and working miracles was his death and resurrection. Jesus showed God's love by being crucified so humans could be forgiven for their wrongdoing.

3. **God the Holy Spirit** – God sent his spirit to Earth after Jesus was taken up to heaven. The book of Acts in the New Testament describes how this happened on the Day of Pentecost. The Holy Spirit shows that God is at work in the world today, to guide and support Christians. In Christian art, the Holy Spirit is often shown as a dove, a symbol of peace and hope.

Belief in the Trinity can be seen in the Bible. In John's Gospel, Jesus said, "The Father and I are one" (John 10:30). Before Jesus returned to Heaven, he instructed his disciples, "Go, then, to all peoples everywhere and make them my disciples: baptise them in the name of the Father, the Son and the Holy Spirit." (Matthew 28:19)

Saint Patrick is said to have used a shamrock to explain the Christian understanding of God to pagans. He made the point that, although there were three leaves, they were still all part of a single stem.

Some people compare the Trinity to the chemical H_2O, which appears as ice when in solid form, water when a liquid and steam when a gas, yet are still the same substance. Although simple symbols can be used to explain the Trinity, it is a complex idea that can be difficult to understand. It is important to remember that Christians are monotheists, meaning they believe in one God, even though this one God has three forms.

> ### KEY TERMS
>
> **The Trinity:** The Christian belief that God can exist in three persons – Father, Son and Holy Spirit.
>
> **Holy Spirit:** The third person of the Trinity; a gift to believers in the early church at Pentecost. The Holy Spirit guides and empowers Christians today.

THE HINDU UNDERSTANDING OF GOD – ONE GOD IN MANY FORMS

In Hinduism there are many different beliefs about God. Hindus believe in one God called Brahman, the power behind everything in the universe and the source of all life. Brahman is everywhere (omnipresent) and is not like anything else in creation (transcendent). Brahman is unknowable to human beings. However, Hindus believe that Brahman reveals himself (knowable) to humans through the thousands of gods and goddesses of Hinduism. When Hindus worship one of these gods, they are really worshipping Brahman.

Hindus believe that the different gods can play a part in people's everyday lives. For example, they might pray to the goddess Lakshmi for help if they have money problems. For Hindus, God is present in every person as an eternal spirit called the *atman*. Hindus believe in reincarnation. When a person attains *moksha* (the final release from the cycle of birth and rebirth), the *atman* reunites with Brahman.

Hindus believe there are three main Gods who work together to keep the universe in balance – Shiva, Vishnu and Brahma. These gods together form the **Trimurti**.

1. **Brahma is the creator**. Brahma is shown in pictures and statues with four faces. He can look north, south, east and west all at the same time to watch over his creation. Brahma is sometimes referred to as grandfather, to show that he has created all the people of the Earth. Brahma is often shown holding a string of prayer beads in one of his four hands. He uses these to keep track of time in the universe he has created.

Krishna

2. **Vishnu is the preserver**. Vishnu sustains Brahma's creation and keeps everything in existence. Hindus believe that Vishnu comes into the world in different forms, often in times of trouble. The different appearances of Vishnu on Earth and called **avatars**. One of the most worshipped avatars of Vishnu is Krishna, a cowherd. He is often shown in pictures playing a flute. Another popular avatar of Vishnu is Rama, a prince married to Sita. They are the main characters in a scripture called **The Ramayana**. So far, here have been nine avatars of the god Vishnu, with a tenth one still to come.

3. **Shiva is the destroyer**. Bringing things to an end is important. For example, winter must end so spring can begin; evil must be destroyed so good can come about; and things must grow old and die so that new life can begin. In statues and pictures, Shiva carries a drum and is often dancing. The rhythm of his dance keeps the universe moving. A circle of flame surrounds Shiva, symbolising the endless cycle of life.

> **KEY TERMS**
>
> **Avatar:** The term used in Hinduism for a god on Earth in the form of a human or animal. It usually refers to one of the ten appearances of Vishnu on Earth.
>
> **Trimurti:** The term referring to the three most important Gods in Hinduism – Brahma, Vishnu and Shiva.
>
> **Ramayana:** A Hindu scripture, telling the story of Rama and Sita.

THE ISLAMIC UNDERSTANDING OF GOD – TAWHID

Muslims believe in one God, Allah, who does not exist in any other form. Muslims call this *tawhid* – the oneness of God. Muslims believe in Allah because they see how good he is when they look at their daily lives and the world around them. Allah is not like anything else that exists and Muslims do not try to describe him (transcendent). Allah is eternal, beyond time and space (omnipresent). He created the world and everything in it, and has a purpose for the world. Allah is perfectly good and loving (omnibenevolent), is interested in how people behave, and wants them to treat each other properly. Muslims also believe that one day Allah will judge everyone.

Muslims believe humans cannot understand Allah, but that he has revealed something of himself to the prophets. Muhammad (570–632 CE) was God's final prophet, an ordinary human being who was chosen by God to deliver his message. Muslims do not worship Muhammad; they respect him as the most important of God's prophets. Muslims believe that Muhammad was visited by the Angel Jibril (Gabriel) on a number of occasions and that the Qur'an was revealed to him. Muslims believe the Qur'an is the complete and final word of God to mankind. By following the teachings of the Qur'an, Muslims can live in a way that is pleasing to God.

Key points

- Belief in one God is the most important belief in Islam. Muslims call this *tawhid* – the oneness of God. The Qur'an states: "Say He is Allah the One … there is none like Him." (Surah 112)
- The *Shahada* is an important statement of faith for Muslims: "There is no God but Allah and Muhammad is the prophet of Allah."
- Muslims call God 'Allah' as this is the Arabic word for God. This word has no gender, nor does it have a plural form.
- In the Qur'an there are 99 names for Allah. Each of these names says something of what he is like, for example, The Creator and The Source of Peace. There is a tradition that the hundredth name for Allah is only known by the camel. This is just a way of saying that human beings can never claim to fully know or understand God.

> **KEY TERMS**
>
> **Tawhid:** The term used to describe the oneness of God in Islam.

AFRICAN TRADITIONAL RELIGION – A POLYTHEISTIC UNDERSTANDING OF GOD

African traditional religion is an example of a polytheistic system of belief. There is a lot of diversity between different countries, but these are some of the key ideas:

- **Belief in mystical powers** – These powers have various names, such as 'dynamism' or 'life force'. In traditional African belief, the source of this power is not always known, but it is associated with the practices of medicine men and women who use natural objects, plants and animals to work charms and magic.
- **Belief in spirit beings** – The spirit world can be broadly divided into two categories: non-human spirits and the spirits of the dead. In African traditional religion, non-human spirits are believed to dwell or inhabit certain trees, rocks, mountains, caves, rivers, lakes, forests, animals, human beings, carved objects, charms and amulets.
- **Belief in gods and a supreme being** – In African traditional religion, there is a supreme being who is the creator and source of all power. Beneath this being, there are many other lesser gods, who must also be worshipped. Lower again in the hierarchy are the spirits of dead relatives, who should also be treated with respect. These ancestors are thought to be closer to the gods as they are dead.

An Introduction to Philosophy of Religion

FURTHER THINKING

Use the Internet to research other belief systems and religions that could be considered polytheistic. Share your findings with others in your class.

QUESTIONS

1. Outline teachings about the nature of God from one world religion you have studied. [5]
2. Explain what one religion you have studied teaches about monotheism. [5]
4. Do you think it is helpful for worshippers to focus on visual images? Give reasons for your answer. [5]
5. "All religions are false as they have different beliefs about the nature of God." Do you agree with this statement? Give reasons for your answer. [5]
6. "There is no point in worshipping God because humans can never know or understand what they are worshipping." Do you agree or disagree? Give reasons for your answer showing that you have considered different points of view. [10]

LEARNING OUTCOMES

Learning outcome	Know & understand	Need to revise	Completed
Ways of understanding and describing God • Immanence • Transcendence • Omnipotent • Omniscient • Omnipresent • Omnibenevolent • Knowable • Unknowable • Monotheism • Polytheism			
Contrasting beliefs about the nature of God • The Christian understanding of God • The Hindu understanding of God • The Islamic understanding of God • A polytheistic understanding of God			

CHAPTER 3

THE PROBLEM OF EVIL AND/OR SUFFERING

Natural suffering and moral evil

Philosophers often make a distinction between two types of evil and suffering:

1. **Natural suffering** – This is suffering caused by nature, such as earthquakes, tornadoes, tsunamis, floods and volcanoes. This type of evil can cause great harm to people, but it is not usually anyone's fault.
2. **Moral evil** – This is evil deliberately caused by the actions of human beings, for example, murder, stealing, lying, war, torture, persecution, genocide, exploitation, poverty and injustice. Moral evil is often a deliberate attempt to harm or upset someone else.

THE DIFFERENCE BETWEEN NATURAL SUFFERING AND MORAL EVIL

> **KEY TERMS**
>
> **Moral evil:** Suffering or pain caused by the acts/words/choices of another person, e.g. murder.
>
> **Natural suffering/natural evil:** Suffering or pain caused by nature, e.g. earthquakes, volcanoes and floods.

Moral evil occurs when someone chooses to go against what the majority of people in society would think of as decent behaviour towards others. Moral evil can also be the result of someone not doing something, such as not helping a person in need when it is within their power to do so. Moral evil happens when someone is acting through their own choice, but it does not have to be a deliberate choice, as moral evil can occur when someone makes a bad decision.

Natural suffering typically includes natural disasters, which some people argue are neither good nor evil; they are just an accepted part of the natural world and no one can be held responsible for them. In some parts of the world, people have to live in areas that can expose them to potential suffering, such as earthquake zones or flood plains. Such natural occurrences might be referred to as '**natural evil**' but they can also bring benefits to humankind. For example, the lava from a volcano produces fertile soils and many people rely on flood water from rivers to irrigate their land.

However, some natural suffering could be the result of human action. For example, some people argue that climate change – leading to drought and starvation in some areas and causing flooding elsewhere – is the result of human action. Others believe the misuse of chemical fertilisers and pesticides could be linked to an increase in certain diseases.

Sickness and disease are other sources of suffering. There are millions of viruses and bacteria in the world that directly cause suffering and death. While some of this suffering might be due to deliberate human action, sickness and disease are usually seen as natural evil.

IN A GROUP

Read the passage below, written by Elie Wiesel, who was a Holocaust survivor.

Working in a group, discuss the answers to the following questions:

1. What did Elie Wiesel witness on his first night in the concentration camp?
2. How has this experience affected him?
3. Elie Wiesel was Jewish and believed certain things about God. Look at the list of God's characteristics below and decide how each of them might have been challenged by what he witnessed in the camp:
   - God is all-loving
   - God is all-powerful
   - God is all-knowing
   - God is present everywhere

'NIGHT' by Elie Wiesel, a Holocaust survivor

"Never shall I forget that night, the first night in the camp, which has turned my life into one long night, seven times cursed and seven times sealed. Never shall I forget that smoke. Never shall I forget the little faces of the children, whose bodies I saw turned into wreaths of smoke beneath a silent blue sky.

Never shall I forget those flames which consumed my faith forever.

Never shall I forget that nocturnal silence which deprived me, for all eternity, of the desire to live. Never shall I forget those moments which murdered my God and my soul and turned my dreams to dust. Never shall I forget these things, even if I am condemned to live as long as God Himself. Never."

From NIGHT, Elie Wiesel

IN A GROUP

Use the Internet to follow the news for a week. Collect examples of news stories by printing or summarising the main stories.

Look at your examples in a group and decide if they show natural suffering or moral evil.

Use your examples to make a group poster.

The origin, nature and purpose of evil and suffering

THE ORIGIN AND NATURE OF EVIL AND SUFFERING

KEY TERMS

Devil/Satan: A term used to describe a personal, spiritual adversary of God, whose aim is to thwart God's purpose and plans.

Free will: The belief that God has given each person the power to perform actions for which he or she is fully responsible; the ability to choose and act on the basis of one's freedom. Christians and Muslims believe that God created humans with free will.

Original Sin: The Christian teaching that everyone is born sinful, with an inclination to do evil. Original Sin is the result of Adam and Eve's disobedience to God.

The Fall: The disobedience of Adam and Eve, resulting in their expulsion from the Garden of Eden.

The Devil or Satan

Through the ages, Christians have associated evil with the Devil or Satan. Satan is the name of the angel who rebelled against God in heaven, so traditionally he is the enemy of God. Satan is often pictured as being red in colour, with horns and a forked tail. Some say he is the source of all the evil in the world. However, not all Christians believe that the Devil is a real person. Some maintain the Devil is a symbolic way of representing the ultimate evil, in opposition to the ultimate good, which is God. To them, Satan is just a word to describe the opposite to God's goodness. If the Devil does exist, it might suggest that God is not all-powerful and cannot control him.

There are references to the Devil in the Bible. In the book of Genesis it is recorded that, in the Garden of Eden, Satan took the form of a serpent and tempted Eve to eat to eat fruit that God had commanded them not to. Some religious believers say this disobedience is the cause of evil and suffering in the world. In the books of Matthew, Mark and Luke, Jesus was led by God into the wilderness to be tempted by Satan. It was a chance for him to face some of the challenges he would encounter during his ministry.

Islam teaches that after God had made Adam, he ordered the angels to bow down to him. Shaytan (the Devil) refused and said that he would tempt humans forever to choose evil rather than good. God allows Shaytan to tempt people (see page 40) and he does this by presenting evil as attractive. However, Shaytan has no power to make people do wrong as God has created everyone with free will.

Free will

As we have seen, suffering is often the result of humans making the wrong choices. Many religions believe that God did not want humans to be like robots, programmed to be loving and obedient towards him. God created human beings who could either choose to love and obey him or disobey and reject him. Christian writer **CS Lewis** wrote that God has created a "live world in which creatures can do real good or harm", not a "toy world which only moves when he pulls the strings." However, this means that some people use their free will to commit evil acts. This is the price to be paid if humans are to become genuinely good creatures.

In the Bible, Adam and Eve exercised their free will and made a deliberate decision to disobey God. Christians believe that because of this disobedience, all humans were separated from God, through sin. The story of Adam and Eve's disobedience in Genesis is known as The Fall. The idea that all people are born with a natural instinct to do wrong is known as Original Sin. Some Christians believe everyone is born with Original Sin. Others prefer to see it as the weakness of human nature. For some people, however, the story of The Fall does not answer all the questions. Surely God knew what would happen if humans were given free will? Why did he not make them perfect so that they would always choose the right thing?

St Augustine believed that God had a plan in allowing humans to have free will and did not abandon them to living in an evil world. God's salvation plan to save humans from evil was to send Jesus to die on the cross so that all sins could be forgiven. As a result, all people have the opportunity to be restored to a right relationship with God.

The human mind

Many people today argue instead that evil has its origin in the human mind. Some people may commit crimes and cause suffering to others because of negative influences in their life, such as their up-bringing or the society they grew up in. Others may have a mental health problem that could make them more likely to commit acts that are seen as evil by the rest of society. For example, when a dreadful crime is reported in the media, the focus is often on what caused such behaviour in the first place, such as parenting, social influences, mental illness, past experiences or trauma.

An important question is: are humans born with a sense of right or wrong, or is it something that develops as they grow? Some people claim that humans are basically evil, needing rules and discipline to keep them on the right track, especially from an early age. However, others argue that people are born good, but can turn bad through unpleasant life experiences.

PHILOSOPHERS AND THINKERS

CS Lewis (1898–1963 CE) was a writer and theologian. He wrote many Christian books and also a series of children's books titled *The Chronicles of Narnia*. He was born in east Belfast and CS Lewis Square in the Connswater area of Belfast pays tribute to him.

St Augustine (354–430 CE) was a Christian theologian and philosopher. He was born in northern Africa, but also lived in Rome. He played an important role in helping Christianity to spread through the Roman Empire.

QUESTIONS

1. (i) What is meant by the term natural evil? [1]
   (ii) Give one example of natural evil. [1]
   (iii) What is meant by the term moral evil? [1]
   (iv) Give one example of moral evil. [1]
   (v) Name the book of the Bible that records the disobedience of Adam and Eve. [1]

2. Explain how human choice can cause suffering in the world. [5]

3. "Satan/the Devil does not exist."
   Do you agree with this statement? Give reasons for your answer. [5]

4. "God should intervene to stop all evil."
   Do you agree or disagree? Give reasons for your answer showing that you have considered different points of view. [10]

The purpose of evil and suffering

Various arguments have been put forward by religious believers to justify why, if God is good, there is evil in the world. These arguments are known as **theodicies**.

SUFFERING IS A TEST

Some people believe that suffering caused by evil is a test from God, to see if people will remain true to their beliefs. A person's faith may be strengthened as a result of a painful experience; someone may learn from the experience and become more mature. Some people say that if people never suffered and never had to choose between right and wrong, then they would be like robots. Some argue that if someone suffers a disaster and loses their faith in God, then surely that faith is exposed as weak and inadequate. If a person's faith remains strong even in the face of extreme difficulty, then they have proved themselves to God. In the Bible, God tested Abraham by asking him to sacrifice his son Isaac as a burnt offering. At the last moment, God sent an angel to stop Abraham. The sacrifice was a test so God knew he could have a covenant with Abraham, based on his faith.

This idea is also important for Muslims and the Qur'an teaches: "And we test you with evil and with good as a trial" (Surah 21:36). **Abu Hamid al-Ghazali** was a famous Muslim philosopher. He argued that God allows people to experience pain as a test of faith. Enduring troubles with strength of character was an important quality that al-Ghazali believed all Muslims should try to develop.

SUFFERING IS A PUNISHMENT FOR HUMAN SIN

Some people believe that God allows people to suffer if they are doing something wrong. This is to make them see the error of their ways and turn back to doing the right thing. In this argument, God uses evil and suffering as an instrument to justly punish human wickedness. In the Bible, Zechariah, the father of John the Baptist, showed a lack of faith when an angel told him that he and his elderly wife would have a son. He was punished by losing his voice until the baby was born. This argument suggests that God uses suffering as an instrument to teach people a lesson.

Hinduism also teaches that suffering is a punishment for human sin, but the punishment may not be immediate. Hindus believe in reincarnation. It is important for each individual to perform good actions, otherwise they will have to suffer in a future life (see 'Hinduism' on page 46.

SUFFERING CAN BUILD STRENGTH OF CHARACTER

Some people believe that suffering is part of God's plan to build people up. At the time, it could be difficult to see a reason for it, but a person might come through a bad experience with a stronger character and more determination. This could be God's intention in allowing people to suffer. People could not be brave if they were never in danger and could not be kind if other people never needed anything. **Irenaeus**, a Christian theologian, argued that God put evil and suffering in the world for a reason, so that people could exercise their freedom and develop as human beings. His ideas are known as the 'soul-making argument'. Irenaeus suggested that God created humans with a soul that was immature but needed to grow and strengthen. This happens through facing up to suffering and challenges in life.

PHILOSOPHERS AND THINKERS

Abu Hamid al-Ghazali (1058–1111 CE) was one of the most famous theologians and philosophers in Islam. He taught at one of the top Madrasas (Islamic place of learning) in Baghdad and was a senior scholar by the age of 33.

Irenaeus (c.130–c.202 BCE) was a Greek bishop who played an important role in guiding Christian communities in what is now the south of France. He also wrote many influential books on Christian theology.

John Hick (1922–2012 CE) was an English writer, philosopher and theologian, who taught in the USA for most of his career. He was a Christian, but some of his views were controversial, such as his belief that Christianity is no more important than any other religion.

Plotinus (c.204–270 CE) was a Greek philosopher who lived in Roman Egypt. He was a vegetarian who believed in living a strict moral life. He believed there was one divine force at work in the world.

John Hick developed this view. He argued that evil and suffering bring out the best in people and help to develop positive qualities, such as courage, love, generosity and compassion. Hick claimed that by experiencing challenges, people become more spiritually mature and grow into the type of person God wants them to become.

In the Bible, Joseph had to suffer by being sold into slavery by his brothers. In Egypt, he was wrongly accused and put in prison. These experiences developed his character and helped Joseph to mature from a spoilt boy to a man full of wisdom with a deep faith in God. Joseph ended up as governor of Egypt, helping his own family and the nation of Egypt to survive a famine.

Only God can see the 'big picture'…

Some Christians believe that no one knows why there is evil in the world or why people suffer. This is something that only God can understand, as only God can see the 'big picture'. When you look at a small part of the universe, it might look like a flawed mess. A violent hurricane or brutal murder might seem like pointless suffering.

However, some religious believers argue that if you could see the big picture, everything would make sense as there is a pattern to the universe and a reason behind everything. This argument maintains that people do not have the right to question God when they do not understand the reason for human suffering. This idea is summed up by Greek philosopher, **Plotinus** who wrote "We are like people ignorant of painting who complain that the colours are not beautiful everywhere in the picture."

Christians believe that God does care about someone when they suffer pain. Because Jesus, God's son, came into the world and died on the cross, God knows what pain is like and shares it with humankind. Sometimes Christians say that when they suffer, they feel closer to God because they know how much they need him. In the Bible, Job had great faith but God allowed Satan to test him. Job lost everything he had. He did not give up his faith, but asked God why he had to suffer so much. Once Job realised that he had to accept what was happening and that God was in control, he received back everything he had lost and more.

However, not everyone agrees that there is a purpose to evil and suffering.

- Why would God need to test the faith of someone who already believed in him? For example, it could be argued that Abraham had already proved his faith in God when he was prepared to leave his home and family.
- Some people have a problem with a loving and forgiving God using human suffering as a way to punish wrong-doing. Also, some people who commit serious crimes seem to get away with what they have done, so it seems to be unfair.
- People do not always learn good things when they suffer pain. Some people become angry and bitter.

- For some people, it is difficult to find a purpose for suffering if it is experienced by, for example, a baby who is too young to learn from the experience or to have committed any wrong-doing.

FURTHER THINKING

Use the Internet to research examples of how people cope when faced with pain and suffering.

How have their experiences affected their faith in God?

The challenge presented by evil and suffering

THE PROBLEM OF EVIL

Do religious beliefs about God make sense when there is so much wrong in the world? It is a fact that evil things happen in the world and millions of innocent people suffer. Some people suggest that if God can work miracles, then he should help when people are suffering or intervene to stop a natural disaster from happening. Some people seem to suffer much more than others, which could raise the question: is God unfair or simply uncaring?

Some people argue that because there is evil and suffering in the world, God does not exist. Or, if there is a God:

- he cannot be loving and good (or he would not allow people to suffer).
- he cannot be completely powerful (or he would use his power to stop evil and suffering).

However, many religious believers maintain that God is completely good (omnibenevolent) and all-powerful (omnipotent). This dilemma is known as **'the problem of evil'**. Many people view 'the problem of evil' as a challenge to the existence of God and religious truth. Some people have reached the conclusion that the existence of evil and suffering makes it impossible to believe that God exists.

Epicurus, a Greek philosopher, argued as follows:
- If God cannot prevent or destroy evil, then he is not omnipotent.
- If God could prevent evil but chooses not to, then he is not omnibenevolent.
- If there was a God who was powerful and good, there would be no evil.
- However, evil exists, therefore there is no God.

This argument put forward by Epicurus is known as the **'inconsistent triad'**, as it is not logical to claim that all three of the following exist at the same time – God who is totally loving, God who is totally good and the presence of evil in the world. Most theists believe in a God who is both powerful and good.

CHALLENGES TO THE EXISTENCE OF GOD AND RELIGIOUS TRUTH

Some people believe that natural suffering presents a direct challenge to the idea that the world was made and is sustained by a good and all-powerful God. The world is cruel: a single hurricane or flood can destroy thousands of lives. There seems to be no sense or justice in the way this suffering is distributed, as it always seems to be the poorest people who suffer from natural disasters, disease or starvation. Some atheists believe that the existence of suffering is proof that God does not exist. They claim that no loving God would let his creations struggle through pain.

KEY TERMS

Atheist: A person who believes that there are convincing reasons and arguments to conclude that God does not exist.

Theist: A person who believes in the existence of God.

Omnibenevolent: Means all-good; it is a quality essential to the nature of God. God is totally loving and the source of all goodness.

Omnipotent: Means all-powerful; it is a quality essential to the nature of God. There is nothing that is beyond God or impossible for him to do.

PHILOSOPHERS AND THINKERS

Epicurus (341–270 BCE) was a philosopher living in Athens in ancient Greece. He believed that seeking small pleasures was the way to a happy life. He wrote over 37 volumes of philosophy but very little remains intact today.

Friedrich Nietzsche (1844–1900 CE) was a German philosopher, composer, poet and writer. He was an atheist and much of his writing was on the topic of good and evil, where he famously declared 'God is dead'.

John Stuart Mill (1806–1873 CE) was a British philosopher and writer who made a huge contribution to social reform. He believed that political and economic decisions should be made on the basis of 'the greatest good for the greatest number of people'.

Some philosophers see natural evil as more of an obstacle to belief in God than moral evil. With moral evil, the blame lies with the people who make bad or evil choices.

Philosopher **Friedrich Nietzsche** observed the world and saw that it was far from perfect and full of flaws. For example, there were earthquakes, floods and volcanoes. He concluded that as there was no natural order or pattern to the world, there was no designer and no God. Nietzsche used the phrase "God is dead" several times throughout his writing.

Philosopher **John Stuart Mill** argued that humans were responsible for many evil things in the world, such as murder, war and torture. However, this was nothing compared to the suffering caused by nature. He wrote "Everything, in short, which the worst men commit either against life or property is perpetrated on a larger scale by nature." Mill concluded that the world was cruel and there was no God in control.

QUESTIONS

1. Describe what is meant by the problem of evil. [5]
2. Outline how Epicurus argued that God did not exist. [5]
3. **Explain how the existence of evil can challenge religious belief. [5]**
4. Do you think pain and suffering can bring benefits to humankind? Give reasons for your answer. [5]
5. "In a world where everyone had enough to live on, there would be no evil."
   Do you agree with this statement? Give reasons for your answer. [5]
6. "All human suffering is a test from God."
   Do you agree or disagree? Give reasons for your answer showing that you have considered different points of view. [10]

THE ISSUE OF INNOCENT SUFFERING

Why does God allow people to suffer? This can be a very difficult question for religious believers to answer. The well-known Christian writer CS Lewis said that the 'problem of pain' was atheism's most potent weapon against the Christian faith.

There are different causes of suffering. Some suffering might be deserved as it is the person's own fault. Perhaps they have broken a rule and need to be punished, or perhaps just been reckless or careless. However, there are some difficult issues to address when it comes to the suffering of the innocent. Why do animals and babies suffer when it is not their fault and they cannot benefit from the experience anyway? Surely it is unfair that some people seem to suffer more than others.

Some possible responses to innocent suffering:

- If we lived in a world where there was no suffering at all, human life would have no meaning, and everyone would be totally dissatisfied. You cannot enjoy pleasure without knowing what it is to experience pain.
- Some people argue that if God has a reason for human suffering, then he should make sure that people do not suffer too much. However, a counter-argument is that if we lived in an easier world where we suffered less, we wouldn't know the difference. Suffering is relative and any amount causes pain.
- Another argument is that how much suffering a person experiences from a painful ordeal all depends on their mental attitude. This might include whether or not they have a strong religious faith. Some people seem to cope with suffering better than others.
- Christianity teaches that no one is innocent. All human beings are naturally sinful and need to repent at some point in their lives. Even babies and young children will make wrong choices as soon as they are old enough to do so.

Case Studies

Dunblane Primary School

On 13 March 1996, Thomas Hamilton carried out the worst school shooting in UK history. Most of the victims were five years old and their teacher was also killed. The gun attack took place in the small Scottish town of Dunblane, near Stirling.

Hamilton, aged 43, was a local resident and a former scout master. However, he was asked to resign as there were complaints about his behaviour towards some of the boys at camp. Before the attack, he was turned down as a voluntary worker for Dunblane primary school. The next day, he shot dead 16 small children and their teacher, and injured 13 others by firing a gun in the school gym. He then turned the gun on himself and took his own life. People who knew Hamilton described him as the kind of person who would become angry and bitter following rejection.

The whole attack took less than three minutes but the children who survived, the victim's families and whole community were left with a lifetime of trauma.

The Aberfan Disaster

On Friday 21 October 1966, a catastrophe occurred in the small Welsh mining village of Aberfan. 116 children and 28 adults lost their lives when they were crushed or drowned in coal slurry. For many years, waste from a nearby coal mine was piled high on the hillside above Aberfan. Disaster struck when more than 150,000 tonnes of coal debris, mixed with water, slid down the hill and engulfed part of the village, killing most of the pupils in Pantglas Junior School. More than 50 years on, residents look back to the tragedy as the mistake that cost a village its children.

It was common practice for the waste from coal mines to be dumped on the hillside and in the 1960s they were a common sight in the valleys of South Wales. However, there was unease about the Aberfan tip, including a petition from Pantglas Junior School in 1963. They asked for the tip to be removed from just behind the school. There was concern that the waste was starting to move, with the situation made worse by underground springs in the area. No action was taken by the authorities.

IN A GROUP

Read the case studies and discuss the following questions:
- What are the differences and similarities between the two tragedies?
- Is one an example of moral evil and the other natural evil? Or is it not as simple as this? Explain your views.
- Do either of these case studies give reasons for denying the existence of God?
- How might a religious believer approach the evil and/or suffering shown in these case studies?

GOD'S PROVIDENCE

Divine providence can be described as God taking an active part in the world. This means God is in control of the whole universe and taking care of everything he has made. In this role, God is all-knowing (omniscient) and always wants what is best for his creation (omnibenevolent). In addition, God is all-powerful (omnipotent) and anything that is logically possible he is able to do. With such a God acting in the world and taking charge of everything, you might expect it to be a perfect place. However, human experience shows that this is far from true. Divine providence is another issue that philosophers have had to deal with when considering the problem of evil and suffering.

John Hick argued that God was not like a pet-owner, who had put humans in a big cage and tried to make life as pleasant as possible with everything provided. Instead, people had to face up to suffering and challenges, making them stronger and more mature. Hick referred to this process as the 'vale of soul-making'.

Case Study
The Lisbon Earthquake

On the morning of 1 November 1755, one of Europe's most powerful earthquakes struck Lisbon, the capital of Portugal. Three shock waves in the space of about ten minutes went through the city. The tremors and the fire that followed destroyed much of the capital. By the end of the week, 75,000 people in Lisbon had died as a direct result of the earthquake, making it one of the worst natural disasters the world has ever experienced.

1 November is All Saints Day, so huge numbers of those who died were in church celebrating the important feast day. Unfortunately, the old construction methods of Lisbon's churches were not designed to withstand violent earth movements and many worshippers died as the roofs of churches collapsed. About half an hour later, people witnessed a strange sight – the sea appeared to have vanished. A huge tsunami wave then destroyed the harbour and thousands of people were swept away and drowned.

What shocked many people was that a lot of the survivors seemed to be those who had no faith. They had not gone to church that morning but had stayed at home. Many people at that time had the view that God would protect those who had faith in him. For the first time, many ordinary people started to question whether there really was a loving and powerful God. The disaster did more than destroy a city and thousands of people. It destroyed the faith of millions of people.

FURTHER THINKING

- Do you think this historical example raises doubts about God's providence?
- Use the Internet to further research the effect of this disaster on people's faith and belief.

The teachings of world religions on evil and suffering

We have already looked at Christian teaching on evil and suffering. Other world religions have different ways of explaining the existence of evil and/or suffering in the world.

HINDUISM

In Hinduism, evil and suffering in the world are not seen as a challenge to the existence of God.

Hindus believe that God contains elements of everything – male and female, birth and death, light and dark, good and evil. Hinduism teaches that every living being has a soul, called the **atman**, which is eternal. Hindus believe in **reincarnation**. When a person dies, their soul will be re-born into another being. In each life, a person does good deeds and bad deeds. Everything a person does will bring its own rewards and punishments. This is called the law of **karma**.

Evil actions build up bad *karma*, which leads to suffering. When people suffer, it is because they have performed bad actions in this life or a previous one. When we look at the world around us, we can see it does not always happen that good people are rewarded for what they do, or that bad people are punished. Hindus believe that the reward or punishment will come in a future life. When bad things happen to people, Hindus do not think it is unfair. Therefore, God cannot be blamed for suffering in the world. Nothing happens by luck or accident and when someone is suffering it is their own fault because of things they have done in the past. Hindus try to cope with evil and suffering by remembering that everything happens for a reason. Coping with suffering bravely and without complaint will help a person have a better life next time.

BUDDHISM

"I teach suffering, its origin, cessation and path. That's all I teach", declared the Buddha 2,500 years ago.

When he was a young man, The Buddha first saw suffering. This caused him to start looking for the meaning of life. He had left the luxury of his father's palace and seen the Four Sights – a sick person, an old person, a corpse and a holy man. The first three made him realise that suffering is part of human life. The sight of the holy man made him think. What is the best way for people to live their lives? What is the point anyway, if people must suffer by getting sick and old and then finally die? Buddha meditated under the Bodhi tree and eventually received **enlightenment** – he could finally understand the origins of suffering and how people can cause less suffering to themselves and others.

The Buddha's teachings about suffering are contained in the **Four Noble Truths** of Buddhism:
- Suffering is a fact of life – everyone must suffer at some stage and it cannot be avoided.
- Suffering is caused when people are greedy and selfish, and want to have too much for themselves, especially material goods.
- Suffering can be reduced by the way people choose to live their lives.
- Following the teachings of Buddhism can help to achieve this.

Humans have a responsibility to avoid evil actions that cause suffering. Most Buddhists believe that the actions and beliefs of human beings such as greed, anger and ignorance give rise to evil and these three things stop Buddhists from reaching enlightenment. Buddhists do not believe that human beings are evil, but they generally accept that humans create suffering through their negative actions.

KEY TERMS

Atman: The term used for the soul in Hinduism; the immortal part of a person that survives death.

Reincarnation: The belief that after death a person's soul is reborn into a new body to live again.

Karma: The result of a person's actions; the idea that every action, good or bad, will bring consequences.

Enlightenment: The state of having knowledge, wisdom or awakened intellect; Buddhists believe a person can become enlightened by following the teachings of the Buddha.

 IN A GROUP

Organise a debate with the motion:

"The existence of evil in the world proves there is no God."

Working in groups of 3 or 4:
- Decide whether your group is for or against the motion.
- Prepare a speech for or against the motion and select a speaker to represent your group to the class.
- Start the debate. Your teacher will select a chairperson to keep order.

RESPONSES TO HUMAN SUFFERING

Some people believe they have a responsibility to care for those in need whatever the cause of their suffering. Witnessing the misery of others can generate a compassionate response and bring out the best in people. Victims of natural disasters, such as drought or floods, depend on others to help them. Christians may support organisations such as Tearfund or Christian Aid, as they remember the teaching of Jesus in the parable of the Good Samaritan. Muslims also place great importance on helping the needy with charitable giving and support for organisations such as Muslim Aid.

Some religious believers try to show compassion even when suffering is the result of human wickedness. One example of someone who put this into practice was Gordon Wilson. His daughter Marie was killed when a bomb exploded in Enniskillen in November 1987. The same evening in a television interview, Gordon said: "We have lost a daughter and I will miss her. But I bear no ill will. I bear no grudge … I pray for these men tonight and every night."

QUESTIONS

1. Describe the teachings of one world religion on coping with evil and suffering. [5]
2. Describe what is meant by God's providence. [5]
3. Explain how a religious faith might help someone to cope with pain and suffering. [5]
4. Do you think religions focus too much on evil? Give reasons for your answer. [5]
5. "When innocent people suffer it is hard to believe in a loving God." Do you agree with this statement? Give reasons for your answer. [5]
6. "Human freedom causes more harm than good." Do you agree or disagree? Give reasons for your answer showing that you have considered different points of view. [10]

An Introduction to Philosophy of Religion

LEARNING OUTCOMES

Learning outcome	Know & understand	Need to revise	Completed
Natural suffering and moral evil • Definition of natural suffering • Examples of natural suffering • Definition of moral evil • Examples of moral evil • The difference between natural suffering and moral evil			
The origin and nature of evil and suffering • Different views of the Devil/Satan • The idea of free will • The human mind			
The purpose of evil and suffering • Suffering is a test • Suffering is a punishment for human sin • Suffering can build strength of character			
The challenge presented by evil and suffering • The problem of evil • Challenges to the existence of God and religious truth • The issue of innocent suffering • God's providence			
The teachings of world religions on evil and suffering • Hinduism • Buddhism • Responses to evil and suffering			

CHAPTER 4

EXPERIENCING GOD

There are many different ways in which humans have claimed to have had an experience of God. This might involve someone feeling that they have personally seen, felt or heard God communicating with them in some way. These experiences vary, from private and personal moments to events where thousands of people are present. Believers who have had a religious experience usually say it has led them to a deeper knowledge or awareness of God. Religious experiences are often positive and encouraging, perhaps leading an individual to lead a better life or help others.

Ways in which believers experience God

1. **Sacred texts** – For many religious believers, their sacred text is seen as the word of God. Therefore, by reading these texts people are able to know something about God and understand what he expects from them.
2. **The examples of religious leaders** – There are many religious leaders (and just ordinary people) who are good examples of how to live for God. By looking at their lives, people can know or experience something of God through them.
3. **Worship** – Religious believers often engage in worship as an act of respect and devotion to God. Worship is a way of honouring God and showing that he is important. Different religions have different ways of worshipping God, such as prayer, singing, fasting or mediation. Through worship, many religious believers feel they can come to know or experience something of God.

> **NOTE:** The specification asks students to look at the different ways in which believers experience God in two world religions. This section looks at three world religions but students only need to learn two of these for the exam.

CHRISTIANITY

How God is revealed through:

1. Sacred texts

By studying the Bible, Christians believe they can learn about God and come to know him. Within the Bible, there are many books containing different types of literature, including history, prophesy, poetry, laws and letters. The Christian Bible is divided into two sections – the Old Testament and the New Testament. It details God's relationship with humankind from the creation of the universe to the spread of Christianity in the first century CE.

Christians believe the Bible is God's word and reveals his teachings. Although the Bible was written over a period of hundreds of years by ordinary people, these people were guided or inspired by the Holy Spirit. Christians believe the message of the Bible is eternal, meaning that it lasts forever. So the Bible is still relevant for Christians today, even though it was written many years ago.

Most Christian worship is based on the Bible. Passages from the Bible are read at every church service, many Christian hymns and songs are based on Bible extracts, and a sermon or homily, based on words from the Bible, is usually given by the person leading the worship. This sermon is used to explain the sacred text, allowing worshippers to understand God's message and how to apply it to their own lives.

Many Christians read the Bible for themselves at home, perhaps using Bible study notes to help them understand what they are reading. Some meet with other Christians in small groups for Bible study.

The Bible explains the nature of God, for example, that God is loving and forgiving, and wants his followers to act in the same way towards others: "God is love, and those who live in love live in union with God and God lives in union with them." (1 John 4:16)

In the Parable of the Unforgiving Servant (Matthew 18:21–35), Jesus taught that God would always forgive a sinner who repented, but in return people must be prepared to forgive each other.

Some Christians feel they can have a personal experience of God through reading the Bible. Someone might read a passage and feel it has a special meaning or message for them, especially if they are going through a tough time, feeling confused or are worried.

The Old Testament was originally written in Hebrew and the New Testament in Greek. The Bible was translated into Latin in the fourth century and first appeared in English in the sixteenth century. At the time of writing, the Bible had been translated into more than 700 languages. Many Bible scholars prefer to study the Bible in its original languages but most Christians think it is important for believers to read the Bible in their everyday language.

2. The example of a religious leader
Mother Teresa
Biographical details

Mother Teresa was born in Yugoslavia in 1910. While still at school she heard about the Loreto nuns who worked in India and applied to join. She believed God was calling her to work among the poorest of the poor. She trained as a nurse, then went to Calcutta to work with people living in the slums. She started a slum school, a home for the dying called Nirmal Hriday, leprosy clinics and children's homes. Mother Teresa organised her sisters into the Missionaries of Charity and their work in Calcutta started to be known throughout the world. Mother Teresa devoted her entire life to helping the poor and needy. She died on 5 September 1997.

Example to others

Mother Teresa's example helps people to experience the love and care that God has for his people. Mother Teresa said, "Be the living expression of God's kindness: kindness in your face, kindness in your eyes, kindness in your smile." Mother Teresa was a true follower of Jesus through her work among the poorest and sickest. She believed that each time she helped someone who was suffering it was as if she was doing it for God: "In each suffering person you can see Jesus". The life and example of Mother Teresa shows that God has a personal interest in the lives of believers (immanent), answering prayer and helping them in daily life through difficulties. Mother Teresa tried to show God's love by helping others and her example has inspired many people to act in similar ways.

3. Worship

Through worship, many Christians experience a God who is immanent and personal. In many churches, a minister, priest or pastor leads people in prayers, hymns and readings from the Bible, and preach a sermon. People who worship in this way feel that the Holy Spirit is active in their worship. They may be filled with a sense of God's presence when in church and that God is speaking directly to them through a prayer, the sermon or a Bible reading. Individual Christians might feel they have been given gifts by the Holy Spirit, such as music, teaching, fundraising or helping people.

Many Christians have a special sense of closeness to God when they take part in Holy Communion, the Lord's Supper, the Eucharist or Mass. They are obeying the command of Jesus to remember his death on the cross by taking bread and wine. Most churches regard this special ceremony as a sacrament. Many Christians feel that they are strengthened by taking part in the ceremony. It is an opportunity to renew their commitment to God.

The Catholic Church teaches that when the bread and wine have been blessed, they become the body and blood of Christ. This is known as Transubstantiation. When Catholics take part in the Eucharist, they may feel they are being nourished by God physically and spiritually.

For Christians, worship means showing respect towards God, the creator of the universe. Through worship, believers can have a direct experience of the omnipotence and transcendence of God.

KEY TERMS

Sacrament: An outward and visible sign of a deeper spiritual reality. Sacraments are practised in Protestant and Catholic churches, e.g. baptism and communion.

Sacred texts: A holy document used by a religion. For example the Bible, which is inspired by God and is believed by Christians to be the final and ultimate source of authority.

Scripture: The holy writings of a religious group which contain guidelines and instructions for living.

Worship: A religious act of adoration; where people are freely expressing and acknowledging the worth of God.

ISLAM

How God is revealed through:

1. Sacred texts

By reading the Qur'an, Muslims believe they can learn what God is like and come to know him. They believe that the Qur'an is the complete and final word of God to human beings. The words of the Qur'an were dictated to the prophet Muhammad by the Angel Jibril and he had to memorise them. These words were later written down exactly as they were given to Muhammad. Therefore, Muslims believe the Qur'an is the direct word of God. The Qur'an was written in Arabic, and most Muslims try to read the Qur'an in this original language. Although it has been translated into other languages, only Arabic copies of the Qur'an are considered to be 'The Holy Qur'an'.

Muslims recite words from the Qur'an during their formal prayers five times a day. Words from the Qur'an are often used to decorate the walls of a mosque. Most Muslim children are taught to read Arabic from an early age so that they can read the Qur'an. During the month of fasting (Ramadan) many Muslims try to read the whole Qur'an from start to finish. A person who can recite the whole Qur'an by heart is called a Hafiz. This is considered a great and worthy achievement.

Muslims can learn how God wants them to live by reading the Qur'an. For example:

- Muslims are told what food is forbidden to them, such as any pork products and meat containing blood.
- How to prepare for prayer.
- What things they are to avoid, such as alcohol and gambling.

2. The example of a religious leader

The Prophet Muhammed

Biographical details

Muhammad is the prophet of Islam. He was born in Mecca in the sixth century CE. He was orphaned at an early age and so knew what it was like to experience suffering and have no one to care for him. Muhammad did various jobs, before finally becoming a trader and travelling with camels across the desert. He had a reputation for being honest and hardworking, so he was given the name 'Al-Amin' meaning 'the trustworthy one'.

When Muhammad was 40 years old, he had the experience that was to change his life. He was praying in a cave when the Angel Jibril appeared to him and said he was to be God's prophet and teach people the ways of Islam. The angel told Muhammad to recite some verses. These were the first verses of the Qur'an, the holy book of Islam. Over a number of years, the whole Qur'an was revealed to Muhammad. Muslims regard him as being the last and final of God's prophets.

Example to others

Through his example, Muhammad revealed to Muslims that there is only one true God. Most people in Mecca at the time were polytheists, but Muhammad set the example of worshipping one God and told the people of Mecca that they were wrong to worship idols.

The example of Muhammad also teaches Muslims how to treat the less privileged in society. Muhammad taught people to work hard and share with others, especially the poor and needy. He showed that God was concerned with justice for all people and in Mecca, he worked to protect the rights of visitors to the city. Therefore, through the example of Muhammad, the less privileged in society could experience God's justice.

3. Worship

Muslims pray five times a day, facing towards the Kaaba in Mecca. Muslim prayer involves moving through different positions, from standing to bowing down with the forehead on the floor. As a mark of respect to Allah, Muslims must pray in a clean area, such as the mosque, or use a prayer mat. Before praying, Muslims perform a ritual washing called wudu, in spiritual preparation for prayer.

Muslims learn a number of things about God through how they worship. Muslims begin prayer by acknowledging God as "compassionate and merciful", so Muslims pray remembering that Allah will forgive their sins. Worshippers' whole bodies are involved in prayer, as Muslims bow and show submission to the will of God. Bowing their faces to the ground is a sign of God's omnipotence. The need for washing and cleanliness shows the transcendence of a Holy God who deserves the greatest respect. Muslims pray all over the world at set times of the day and through their worship share an experience of God who is immanent and omnipresent, is active in the world, and hears their prayers.

HINDUISM

How God is revealed through:

1. Sacred texts

There are many sacred writings in Hinduism, composed over thousands of years. By reading sacred texts, Hindus believe they can learn what God is like. These are some of the most important for Hindus:

The Vedas are the most ancient Hindu texts, dating back to 1200 BCE. These texts are sometimes called *shruti*, meaning 'heard'. Hindus believe the Vedas were received by scholars direct from God and passed on to the next generation by word of mouth. *Shruti* texts therefore give a direct message from God. The Vedas contain hymns of praise to God, prayers and rituals to guide Hindu priests and chants for worship and meditation.

The Upanishads are also *shruti* and contain the philosophical teachings of Hinduism. Central teachings in the Upanishads are the ideas of Brahman, the universal power, and the *atman*, the individual soul.

The Bhagavad Gita is one of the most popular Hindu scriptures. It is known as a *smriti* text, meaning 'remembered'. These texts are important but are not considered to come directly from God. They are thought to be the product of the minds of great Hindu thinkers. The Bhagavad Gita is written as a form of a dialogue and explains Hindu belief about the immortality of the soul and reincarnation.

The Ramayana is also a *smriti* text and contains one of the most popular stories in Hinduism. It tells how Prince Rama and his wife Sita were exiled to a forest, where Sita was abducted by the evil demon Ravana. The main theme is how good will always triumph over evil. It is also a story about duty, with Rama and Sita held up as role models for the perfect husband and wife.

Hindus believe that God is revealed directly through *shruti* texts but they can also learn important Hindu teachings in the *smriti* texts.

2. The example of a religious leader
Mahatma Gandhi

Biographical details

Mohandas Gandhi was born in British-ruled India in 1869. His family sent him to England to study law, where he became interested in the philosophy of non-violence. He was partly inspired by Hindu teachings and also Jesus' Sermon on the Mount in the Bible. After qualifying as a lawyer, Gandhi went to South Africa for a year, where he developed his ideas of non-violent resistance. By the time he returned to India, he had earned admiration for his willingness to endure prison and punishments for the sake of justice. People started to call him 'Mahatma' or 'great soul'.

At home in India, Gandhi started to organise non-violent protests against the British rulers in India. These included marches, strikes and non-cooperation with unjust laws. He spent time in prison, but eventually his efforts helped to free India from British rule. Gandhi was assassinated by a Hindu nationalist in Delhi in 1948. His death was mourned as the loss of one of India's greatest heroes.

Example to others

Through his leadership, Gandhi gave many important lessons for others to follow. One of the main features of all his campaigning was the principle of peaceful resistance. Although Gandhi was open to the teachings of other religions, he firmly maintained the Hindu idea of *ahimsa* or non-violence. Another inspiring feature of Gandhi's leadership was his desire to help others and stand up for people who were oppressed.

Through his campaigns against injustice, Gandhi showed both will power and perseverance. He was insulted, jailed and beaten, but he refused to give in. He said, "First they ignore you, then they laugh at you, then they fight you, then you win." Gandhi knew that he wanted to change India and he was determined to achieve this. He told his followers, "You must be the change you wish to see in the world". Gandhi believed that Hinduism involved the pursuit of non-violence and justice. Through his leadership and example, he reinforced these principles and showed his followers that this was how God wanted them to live.

> ### 🎓 FURTHER THINKING
> Use the Internet to research other religious leaders who provide examples for others to follow. Examples could include Martin Luther King, Guru Nanak, The Dalai Lama and Pope Francis. Make sure you explain how God is revealed through the life of each person.

3. Worship

Hindu worship, known as *puja*, involves the use of all five senses – sight, smell, touch, taste and sound. A statue or image, known as a *murti*, is essential in Hindu worship, whether the devotions are taking place at home or in the temple. Hindus do not worship these statues but use them as a visual point to concentrate on when worshipping. Sometimes the *murtis* are anointed with red paste or kissed as a sign of respect. A Hindu shrine will often be very colourful, with flowers and fruits as offerings.

Hindu worship often involves chanting, such as repeating the sacred sound 'Om' or saying a *mantra*, (a phrase or prayer), usually in Sanskrit. Sometimes passages from scriptures are read or chanted. Other sounds might include blowing a conch shell or ringing a bell. During Hindu worship, incense is burned as a sign of respect, as it is believed to clean the air and bring a pleasant smell to the shrine. After *puja* has taken place, Hindus often share the food offered to the god after they have worshipped. This food is called *prasad*, meaning 'edible gift'.

Through worship, many Hindus experience a God who is personal and immanent. As they worship at a shrine, perhaps mediating or focusing on an image, they will feel God's presence and strength. However, as humans can never understand Brahman (the Great Power) they are also reminded that God is transcendent and impersonal. The use of all the senses in Hindu meditation reminds Hindus that Brahman is omnipresent. He is active in every aspect of the universe and in their everyday lives.

> ### 🐟 IN A GROUP
> Discuss the following questions in small groups:
> - Which give the best example to follow – religious leaders or sacred texts?
> - Is it preferable to read sacred texts in their original language?

QUESTIONS

1. Describe how a religious believer might experience God through worship in one world religion you have studied. [5]
2. Outline the importance of sacred texts in one world religion you have studied. [5]
3. Explain what religious believers might learn about God from the example of a religious leader. [5]
4. Do you think sacred texts should be read in their original language? Give reasons for your answer. [5]
5. "Ancient religious writings no longer have relevance for today's world."
   Do you agree with this statement? Give reasons for your answer. [5]
6. "Personal religious experiences cannot be used as evidence that God exists."
   Do you agree or disagree? Give reasons for your answer showing that you have considered different points of view. [10]

The nature and importance of revelation

Revelation describes how religious believers come to a deeper understanding of God through personal experience. Revelation comes from the word 'reveal' which means to show something that was previously hidden. In this case, God is revealed to believers in a more meaningful way, or in a way that leads a person to have a faith. There are many ways to experience God and religious believers do not all have the same experiences to bring them closer to God.

GENERAL REVELATION

This is the way that God reveals himself through things that anyone can see and understand if they are interested. It is indirect and available to every person and in every place. God is revealed through the natural and physical world, reasoning and human conscience.

God may reveal himself through a holy book which anyone can read. Anyone who chooses to do so can study the life of a religious leader and learn something about God or how God wants people to live. Some people say that general revelation can come from the beauty of the natural world that God has created; again, this is something that is open to everyone to witness. A person's conscience, their sense of right and wrong, can also be general revelation. Some people see their conscience as the voice of God telling them when they have done wrong.

SPECIAL REVELATION

Special revelation is directly targeted at specific people in a particular time and place. It is a highly personal experience and might take place through a vision, dream or visit from an angel. Special revelation also includes God working miracles, perhaps in answer to prayer. A special revelation is often dramatic and life-changing for the person involved. People who experience special revelation often feel that God is calling them to do a particular task. Judaism, Christianity and Islam have all claimed that the teachings of certain prophets or holy people are the results of special revelation. These experiences come from a very personal God, concerned about his creation. Both the Bible and the Qur'an emphasise the importance of dreams and visions as special revelations from God.

Many Hindus believe that through meditation they can gain a deeper knowledge of Brahman. This is also an example of special revelation as it is a personal experience. Hindus may meditate through repeating the sacred sound 'Om', chanting religious verses or using a string of prayer beads to focus the mind.

ACTIVITY

Look at the spider diagram below.
Which are examples of general revelation and which are special revelation?
Are there any that could be both?

KEY TERMS

General revelation: Knowledge of God available to everyone, e.g. through reflection on nature.

Special revelation: Knowledge of God that is not available to everyone, but rather to an individual or a group of people. Dreams, visions, prophecies and miracles can all be regarded as special revelation by Christians. Reading the Bible is also special revelation when a believer feels God is speaking specifically to them.

Conversion: The process of a person changing from one belief/religion to another, e.g. someone who changes from being a Muslim to a Christian.

CAN REVELATION LEAD TO RELIGIOUS FAITH?

Some religious believers claim that God meets with them directly, through worship or prayer. They might feel the presence of God when they are praying, or have a prayer answered. For someone receiving these special revelations, God is a personal and living God. Sometimes a person who was formerly an unbeliever has an experience like this, which has led to a religious faith. This is often referred to as a religious conversion.

Not all religious believers have a dramatic conversion experience. Writer **CS Lewis'** conversion is an example of an intellectual conversion. Lewis describes how he talked for hours with his friend, the author JRR Tolkien, who was an Christian. As a result of these conversations, he became convinced of the truth of Christianity. **St Augustine** is an example of a moral conversion. He changed his lifestyle when confronted by the challenge of living a moral Christian life. His conversion was not a sudden change, but a gradual process.

Some people have a point in their life when they turned to faith that does involve a direct experience of God. A well-known example from the Bible is the conversion of Saul on the road to Damascus (see page 63). A more recent example is that of Nicky Cruz, a notorious New York Gang leader.

Case Study
The conversion of Nicky Cruz
Nicky Cruz (born 1938) was the leader of a vicious gang called the Mau Maus. He was involved in drugs, murder and other criminal activities. He met David Wilkerson, a Christian preacher, who told Nicky that Jesus loved him. Nicky responded by slapping David and threatening to kill him. David, just smiled and prayed for Nicky. Two weeks later, Nicky attended a meeting led by David. He felt overwhelmed with guilt and prayed with David for God's forgiveness. Nicky became a Christian, started to study the Bible and eventually became a preacher himself. For more than 50 years, Nicky Cruz has travelled the world, preaching the Christian message to people of all ages and backgrounds.

Examples of revelation

In this section, we will consider examples of revelation from sacred texts, history and the modern world.

SACRED TEXTS
The Prophet Muhammad
Look at the details given about Muhammad's life on page 52.

Muhammad continued to have visits from the Angel Jibril for the rest of his life, as the whole of the Qur'an was gradually revealed to him. Muslims believe that Muhammad also had other direct experiences of God. One example is called 'The Night Journey'. Muhammad had a vision where he travelled on a winged horse to Jerusalem. He then met with God and toured heaven and hell, meeting prophets such as Abraham and Moses.

The Call of Isaiah (Isaiah 6:1–8)
The Old Testament book of Isaiah describes how Isaiah was called by God to be a prophet. The passage describes, in Isaiah's own words, the vision he had of God when he was in the temple:

> In the year that King Uzziah died, I saw the Lord. He was sitting on his throne, high and exalted, and his robe filled the whole Temple. Around him flaming creatures were standing, each of which had six wings. Each creature covered its face with two wings, and its body with two, and used the other two for flying. They were calling out to each other:
>
> "Holy, holy, holy! The LORD Almighty is holy! His glory fills the world."
>
> The sound of their voices made the foundation of the Temple shake, and the Temple itself became filled with smoke. I said, "There is no hope for me! I am doomed because every word that passes my lips is sinful, and I live among a people whose every word is sinful. And yet, with my own eyes I have seen the King, the LORD Almighty."
>
> Then one of the creatures flew down to me,

carrying a burning coal that he had taken from the altar with a pair of tongs. He touched my lips with the burning coal and said, "This has touched your lips, and now your guilt is gone, and your sins are forgiven." Then I heard the Lord say, "Whom shall I send? Who will be our messenger?"

I answered, "I will go! Send me!"

Following this experience, the Old Testament records how Isaiah delivered God's message to the people of Israel.

FROM HISTORY

John Wesley

John Wesley (1703–1791 CE) is remembered as the founder of the Methodist Church. Although he had a religious upbringing and tried to live by Christian principles, he was very unsure of his faith. In 1738, John Wesley had a very real and personal experience of God:

> "In the evening I went very unwillingly to a meeting in Aldersgate Street [in London], where one was reading Luther's preface to the Epistle to the Romans. About a quarter before nine, while he was describing the change which God works in the heart through faith in Christ, I felt my heart strangely warmed. I felt I did trust in Christ, Christ alone for salvation; and an assurance was given me, that he had taken away my sins, even mine, and saved me from sin and death."

After this experience of God, John Wesley spent the rest of his life preaching the message of Christianity. He travelled all round Britain and Ireland, covering over 250,000 miles on horseback.

THE MODERN WORLD

Religious experiences continue to be important in a modern, scientific age. In the twentieth and twenty-first centuries, many people claim to experience God in a variety of ways, through conversion experiences, miracles, visions and prayer.

One example is Healing on the Streets (HOTS), a Christian ministry that began in Coleraine, Northern Ireland in 2005. HOTS believes that the power of prayer can heal. It takes its ministry out onto the streets, inviting people to sit down on a chair and be prayed for. Through this simple approach, HOTS says that many people are healed in various ways. Some people are cured from physical pain and illnesses, while others find healing through a sense of inner peace and calm. Some people are healed instantly, and some come back regularly to be healed over a period of time. The Christian volunteers working on a HOTS team believe that God always touches the lives of people when they come for prayer. The initiative has now spread to over 700 churches in 17 countries.

IN A GROUP

Look at the examples of religious experience above and discuss the following questions:

- In what ways was each experience life changing for the person involved?
- Was this experience life changing for others?
- Can any of these experiences be proved?

FURTHER THINKING

- Use the Internet to find other examples of religious experience in the modern world.
- Have any of these experiences led to religious faith, or were those involved already believers?

NOTE: 'The Argument from Religious Experience' in Chapter 1 (page 12) looked at the experiences of Saul and Moses. These are also relevant here as examples of special revelation.

ANSWERED AND UNANSWERED PRAYER

Praying is a powerful way of asking for God's help with anything from a personal issue to a world disaster. Answered prayer is when the outcome someone has been praying for takes place. Unanswered prayer is when nothing happens or when God seems to be saying "No".

Christians believe that God hears all prayers and will respond as he sees best, even if they seem to be

unanswered at the time. Many Christians believe they have a religious experience each time they pray as they are developing a relationship with God.

Many Christians claim to have experienced God's power and involvement in their lives through answered prayer. Prayer is all about faith. Prayers being answered can strengthen faith and also lead to the religious conversion of an unbeliever. Prayer has power in providing comfort to those who need it, direction for people in need of guidance and answers for those who seem lost. Also important for believers is accepting that unanswered prayer is God's way of saying that something is not in his plans.

Some philosophers have argued that unanswered prayer calls God's omnipotence or omnibenevolence into question, as it suggests that God is not powerful enough or loving enough to answer prayer. Unanswered prayer can present a challenge to belief in God:

- If sincere prayers go unanswered, people may doubt that there is a God to answer them.
- Some people may conclude that God does not care about them, resulting in loss of faith.
- Atheists might use unanswered prayer as evidence of God's non-existence.

In his book *The God Delusion* Richard Dawkins argued that there is almost certainly no God and that belief in a personal God is a delusion. He referred to an experiment carried out on the effects of prayer in 2006. In 'The Great Prayer Experiment', three churches in America prayed for 1,802 patients under-going heart surgery. Some patients received prayer and others did not. The churches who prayed for patients could do so in any way they wanted to but had to use the phrase 'successful surgery with a quick, healthy recovery and no complications'.

The experiment showed that there was no difference between the patients who received prayer and those who did not. It has been used by atheists, such as Dawkins, as evidence that God does not exist.

However, some religious believers might claim that it is impossible to study prayer in an experiment, as God does not respond to challenges. Others take 'Do not put the Lord your God to the test' (Deuteronomy 6:16) to mean that prayer should not be examined in this way and dismiss the results of the experiment.

KEY TERMS

Miracle: An extraordinary event that cannot be explained by natural or scientific laws. It is usually regarded as a direct action of God and provides evidence for his existence.

Prayer: A way in which people communicate with God either personally or as a group.

MIRACLES

Miracles are an example of special revelation. However, they are different to some of the other ways of experiencing God. Miracles are not private things going on inside someone's head. If they happen at all, then they happen in the real world, so this should make them easier to prove. Do miracles really happen? If they do, are miracles proof that God exists?

St Augustine was a famous Christian philosopher who lived in the fourth century. He believed that miracles really happen and are a sign from God. For the next thousand years, most philosophers agreed with Augustine.

Thomas Woolston lived in Britain in the eighteenth century. He wrote a book in which he argued that miracles were not true. He also described the resurrection of Jesus as a 'bare-faced fraud' committed by the disciples. Woolston was found guilty of blasphemy and fined. He could not afford to pay so was sent to prison and died there four years later.

Scottish philosopher **David Hume** also lived in the eighteenth century. He too argued that miracles were not true but he was never arrested, as he wrote his ideas in secret and they were not published until after his death. He said that events simply could not happen if they went against a law of nature. If a few people claimed to have witnessed an event that went against the laws of nature, did that mean that a miracle had taken place? Hume argued is more likely that the witnesses got it wrong.

William Paley (who is associated with the Argument from Design) disagreed with Hume and wrote a book to try and prove him wrong. Paley did not claim that miracles were true but argued that there were very good reasons for believing in them. One reason was that if there was a God then it was quite likely that he would interrupt the laws of nature from time to time to make something happen. Paley also claimed that the resurrection of Jesus was a historical fact, as the disciples were honest witnesses. They would not have been prepared to die for something they had made up.

PHILOSOPHERS AND THINKERS

Richard Dawkins (1941–) is a British evolutionary biologist, author and broadcaster. He is well known for his atheist views and criticisms of religion.

Thomas Woolston (1668–1733) was an English theologian who held some controversial religious views, that led to him being in trouble with the authorities. He believed that the Bible should not be taken literally and denied that Jesus performed miracles in the Gospels.

Rudolf Otto (1869–1937) was a German theologian, philosopher and historian. He was a Christian and his ideas on what it meant to experience something holy had worldwide impact.

Miracles in the Bible

It can be very difficult to prove whether an event described thousands of years ago actually happened. Some people do not accept all the miracles described in the Bible, preferring to find a more rational explanation. However, for Christians who take everything in the Bible as literal truth, the miracles happened just as described. Most Christians view the miracles in the New Testament very positively. These miracles were written down within living memory of the people who witnessed them. There are two miracles that are essential for Christian belief – the incarnation (when God took on human form in the person of Jesus) and the resurrection (when God raised Jesus from the dead).

Nearly a third of Mark's Gospel describes miracles, so there was a strong tradition that Jesus' miracles did happen. However, there is still the difficulty of providing physical evidence and so some people remain sceptical.

The continuing importance of miracles

For many Christians today, dramatic miracles do not form a part of their religious experience. They accept the miracles in the Bible but say that they do not happen today in the same way. Some Christians argue that since the Bible was written God does not need to show himself in the world in a dramatic way. People can experience God's power through his word. However, others disagree and claim that God still works miracles today.

Some people would argue that just because science cannot explain apparently miraculous healings, it does not prove that God is involved. There may be a perfectly rational explanation that we are not aware of. Others argue that the human mind can have a powerful impact on the body. A psychosomatic healing is one where a person imagines they have

IN A GROUP

Organise a debate with the motion:

"Miracles happen today and they are evidence that God exists."

Working in groups of 3 or 4:

- Decide whether your group is for or against the motion.
- Prepare a speech for or against the motion and select a speaker to represent your group to the class.
- Start the debate. Your teacher will select a chairperson to keep order.

Experiencing God

Case Study
Lourdes, France

In 1858, a 14-year-old girl called Bernadette Soubirous claimed to have experienced a number of visions of the Virgin Mary. On one of these occasions she was asked by the Virgin to drink from a small spring. She could not see any water, but dug in the Earth until a bubbling pool appeared. A chapel was built here and the underground spring is believed to have healing powers. More than five million pilgrims visit Lourdes every year in hope of a cure, either for themselves or others. The Church has established an International Medical Committee at Lourdes to check the validity of these miraculous claims. This only happens after all possible scientific explanations have been ruled out. One example is the case of Jean-Pierre Bely, who was diagnosed as having multiple sclerosis in 1984. His friends took him to Lourdes and even though he had not been able to walk for two years. Within a few days he could walk, run and ride a bike. After twelve years of detailed examination, the Church declared the cure to be a miracle.

been made well, because they have so much faith in God's power to heal. Sceptics claim that these healings are not permanent, and the symptoms return after a time.

On the other hand, many religious believers argue that, with many people claiming to have experienced miracles, can they all be wrong? If God is all-powerful, then miracles are well within his ability. For example, there may be accounts of patients recovering when medical experts have given up hope.

VISIONS

Some believers claim to have experienced God through a vision. Some have had a dream-like experience in which God is speaking to them. A religious vision is often a turning point in someone's life. There are many examples in the Bible, for example, an angel appeared to Mary and tells her she will give birth to God's son. Muslims believe the angel Jibril appeared to Muhammad on a number of occasions and revealed the Qur'an to him.

Case Study
Knock Shrine, Ireland

In 1879, Mary McLoughlin, the housekeeper of the parish priest of Knock, County Mayo, saw the south wall of the church bathed in light. There was an image of the Virgin Mary, St Joseph and St John. She ran to a friend's house to tell what she had seen. More than a dozen people saw the image, which lasted for about three hours before it faded away. Witnesses say the figures were fully rounded, as if they had a body and life. They did not speak and seemed to float about two feet from the ground. At first, the church authorities were sceptical, but more and more people began to visit and there were reports of miraculous healings. Knock has become a centre for over half a million visitors each year, making pilgrimages to honour the vision or to ask for healing.

THE NUMINOUS

The word numinous comes from Latin and means 'divine power'. Many testimonies from those claiming to have had a religious experience describe a sense of being in the presence of something greater

than them, yet feeling distinctly separate from it. German theologian Rudolf Otto used the term 'numinous' to refer to being in the presence of an awesome power. He wanted to identify what it was about a religious experience that made it a special experience. Otto suggested that many of the visions recorded in the Bible, such as Moses' encounter with God at the burning bush, are experience of the numinous.

>  **FURTHER THINKING**
>
> There are many ways that religious believers can experience God. For example, many believers have an experience of God through a pilgrimage to an important religious site. Others believe that God can be revealed through caring for others or performing acts of charity. Use the Internet to research these and other possible ways of experiencing God.

Challenges to religious experience

Special revelations are difficult for religious believers to explain to others who do not share their faith. These revelations are generally only experienced by one person, so believing they are genuine usually requires faith. General revelation is a way in which some religious believers experience God through features of everyday life, such as an appreciation of the natural world or knowing the difference between right and wrong. However, non-religious people argue that these can be explained easily without reference to God. For example, science can explain the beauty and complexity of the natural world. People know what is right and wrong, and behave in a morally acceptable way, because this is better for everyone in society. It is not because God has given people a sense of moral duty.

Religious experiences can raise many difficulties:

THE EXPERIENCE IS A HALLUCINATION

Some religious believers claim to have experienced visions, which are often accompanied by voices. The prophet Muhammad receiving the Qur'an from the angel Jibril was a vision experience, accompanied by hearing God's words spoken through the angel. St Bernadette described a vision of the Virgin Mary at Lourdes, in which she could recall what the Virgin Mary had been wearing and the words she spoke. The difficulty with these experiences is proving that they really happened.

For the person who has a religious experience, it is real for them. However, religious experiences remain difficult to prove to those who have never had them, and they are often dismissed as lacking in credibility. A person may have an unreliable memory of the experience, may have misunderstood what was happening, or simply be making everything up.

A person's experience might happen only in their mind, but it could still be a real experience that God has caused to happen. God can be experienced through the mind, the senses and through nature. This can happen through prayer, meditation or taking part in a religious ritual. People have had experiences of God throughout time and in greatly varying cultures and faiths. Surely, believers argue, these people cannot all be wrong or deluded?

THE EXPERIENCE IS THE RESULT OF WISH-FULFILMENT

Psychologist **Sigmund Freud** believed that religious experience could be explained by psychological factors acting on a person's personality. Freud thought the human condition was one of fear in the face of death, and helplessness in the face of nature.

Therefore, people needed comfort: as children this came from a human father, later in religion the father-in-the-sky. Freud described this religious comfort as wish-fulfilment. Freud believed that powerful wishes could find outlets in dreams, and also in religious visions, voices and other religious experiences. They were not 'real' but illusions coming from a powerful need for people to feel control over their own helpless state.

KEY TERMS

Hallucination: An experience involving the apparent perception of something that is not actually present at the time.

Illusion: A false belief that is not justified or warranted but which possesses a certain quality that suggests to some people that it is true.

Numinous: Having a deeply religious or spiritual experience, sometimes triggered by being in a particular place or situation.

Vision: Something that is seen in a dream or dream-like state and regarded by the subject as a revelation from God.

LACK OF EVIDENCE FOR RELIGIOUS EXPERIENCE

Sceptics (people who doubt) claim that religious experiences are the product of the human mind and do not relate to reality. They say that such experiences are illusions, as only the things people we experience with their senses are real. However, for people who have had experiences, or who take a spiritual view of life, such things are real. For example, St Bernadette testified that the Virgin Mary had spoken to her. Yet witnesses to the experience stated that they did not see or hear the Virgin Mary and only saw Bernadette talking to an 'unseen' someone. Sceptics would claim that there is no way of proving that having a vision or hearing voices are genuine or have come from God.

Is a religious phenomenon more believable if many people experience it together, at the same time? The effects of such an experience can be life changing, suggesting it should be taken as credible. On the other hand, sceptics suggest that with large groups of people, it is more likely to be a form of mass hysteria, as everyone wants to join in and be part of something.

Case Study
The Toronto Blessing

The Toronto Blessing refers to a Christian revival movement that began in January 1994. Members of the Toronto Airport Vineyard Church reported feeling the presence of the Holy Spirit. This often affected them in dramatic ways, including uncontrollable laughter, shaking, paralysis or falling down as if in a deep sleep. The first time this happened in the church, there were about 120 people at the meeting. Over the following year, the church's size increased to 1000 members with meetings held almost every night of the week. The revival spread to other churches worldwide, with people experiencing similar affects.

 **FURTHER THINKING**

- Use the Internet to find out more about the Toronto Blessing.
- Do you think that many thousands of people having the same experience over several years is sufficient to prove a religious experience is genuine?
- Research other examples of several people having a shared religious experience. To what extent do you consider these examples to be genuine?

Some questions to consider

1. Why does God allow some people to have a religious experience and not others?

This is a difficult question, as it could seem as if God is choosing some people to have a special experience which is denied to others. Surely this cannot be fair, or the way a loving and compassionate God would work? Religious believers would respond that general revelation is open to everyone, but some people never have a religious experience. This could be because they do not believe in anything spiritual and so are not receptive to seeing God at work in their lives or the world around them. Many religious believers would also say that God has a plan for everyone. It could be that some people need to be told in a very clear and dramatic way what God wants them to do, and this results in a special revelation. For others, a special revelation may occur because they are close to God through a life of worship, prayer or meditation. Perhaps everyone will have an experience of God at some stage in their lives but not everyone will recognise it as such.

2. Does a religious experience prove that God exists?

For a sceptic, who only believes in physical experiences felt through the senses, accounts of religious experiences will not be convincing. They might argue that, in the past, comets, eclipses and even the rainbow were seen as supernatural messages sent from God. We now know they are entirely natural events with a scientific explanation. Perhaps all claims to special revelation from God will eventually be seen in the same way? Sceptics might also argue that personal and private experiences of God, such as visitations or miraculous healings, do not stand up to scientific scrutiny. Therefore, they cannot be used to prove the existence of God. People may be mistaken or hallucinating. Religious experiences can often seem very real, but how does a person know that they have had an experience of God and not some other supernatural force?

However, others claim that religious experiences are proof of God's existence. An important point to consider is what happens following a religious experience. Often, it results in a completely changed life. For example, in the New Testament, Saul, a righteous Jew, was travelling to Damascus to arrest Christians. On the way he had a personal experience of God that led to his conversion to Christianity. He spent the rest of his life preaching about the religion he tried to stamp out, and was one of the greatest missionaries in the Church. Many people would conclude from Paul's story that religious experience is the most powerful argument for the existence of God.

> **NOTE** 'The Argument from Religious Experience' in Chapter 1 (page 12) contains further arguments about whether religious experiences can be used to prove the existence of God.

QUESTIONS

1. Describe an example of revelation from a religious text. [5]
2. Outline why some people claim there is no evidence for religious experience. [5]
3. Explain the difference between general and special revelation. [5]
4. Do you think it is difficult to experience God in the modern world? Give reasons for your answer. [5]
5. "God always answers prayer." Do you agree with this statement? Give reasons for your answer. [5]
6. "Miracles are simply coincidences. There is always another explanation." Do you agree or disagree? Give reasons for your answer showing that you have considered different points of view. [10]

LEARNING OUTCOMES

Learning outcome	Know & understand	Need to revise	Completed
Ways in which believers experience God • Christianity - Sacred texts - The example of religious leaders - Worship • Islam - Sacred texts - The example of religious leaders - Worship • Hinduism - Sacred texts - The example of religious leaders - Worship			
The nature and importance of revelation • General revelation • Special revelation • Revelation and religious faith			
Examples of revelation • Sacred texts • History • The modern world • Answered and unanswered prayer • Miracles • Visions • The numinous			
Challenges to religious experience • Hallucination • Wish-fulfilment • Lack of evidence			

CHAPTER 5
LIFE AFTER DEATH

The teachings of world religions on the afterlife

Most religions teach that there is some form of afterlife and the idea of a soul, the spiritual part of a human that can survive death.

> **NOTE**
> The specification asks students to look at two different ways in which world religions understand the afterlife. This section looks at three world religions but students only need to learn two of these for the exam.

CHRISTIANITY

Christianity teaches that death is not the end and that there is an afterlife. However, Christians believe no one can fully understand what this life after death will be like. There are teachings in the Bible but it is impossible to know exact details.

The resurrection of Jesus

Jesus' resurrection gives Christians hope for eternal life. The New Testament teaches that Jesus, the Son of God, died on the cross and was raised to life by God. This makes it possible for those who have faith in him to have their sins forgiven and go to heaven when they die. The resurrection of Jesus proves there will be an afterlife. In John's Gospel, Jesus said:

> "I am the resurrection and the life. Those who believe in me will live, even though they die; and those who live and believe in me will never die." (John 11:25–26)

Jesus promised his followers they would have eternal life. The resurrection proves that God is able to make this possible as he is more powerful than death.

The soul

Christians believe that each person has a soul. The soul cannot be seen, never dies, and it makes people different from every other kind of animal. At creation, humans were made in God's image:

> "So God created human beings, making them to be like himself. He created them male and female." (Genesis 1:27)

Many Christians think this means that God put something of his own nature in each person. There is a part of every human that is immortal, that is, will live on forever. Christians believe that human life is very valuable to God, as people have souls that will survive when the body dies. A soul makes each person special and unique.

Judgement

Christians believe that God will judge people on both their faith and their actions. Some Christians believe that this will happen when they die, while others believe there will be a Judgement Day at the end of time, when everyone is judged. Some Christians believe that judgement will be in two stages: an initial judgement when a person dies, followed by the final judgement at the end of time.

The Bible teaches that this final judgement will happen when Jesus returns to Earth for a second time. This event is sometimes called the **Parousia**. When Jesus comes to Earth again, he will not return as a baby, born in humble surroundings, like the first time; he will come in glory to judge the world. After this judgement, people will spend eternity in either heaven or hell.

Heaven and hell

Most Christians believe that when they die, the body is not needed any more. For those who have followed God's way on Earth, their soul will go to heaven. This is seen as a place free of suffering where they will spend eternity with God. There are different beliefs among Christians about hell. Some Christians believe that hell is a real place, full of pain and suffering. In the past, the idea of hell was often used to encourage people to be morally good for fear of ending up there after death. However, some Christians believe that the biblical descriptions of hell are symbolic to help people to understand what it could be like to live for eternity without God.

Some Christians, particularly Catholics, also believe in **purgatory**, a place between heaven and hell. Most people are probably not good enough to go straight to heaven because of the sins they have committed on Earth but they have believed in Jesus so they will not go to hell. Instead, their souls go to purgatory where they are punished for a time, to cleanse them of sin, before they are able to enter heaven.

> **KEY TERMS**
>
> **Resurrection:** The act of being raised from the dead. In Christianity, this refers to the resurrection of Jesus by God and also the resurrection of believers to eternal life.
>
> **Soul:** The spiritual or immaterial part of a human being that continues to exist after a person has died. The soul is the essential part of someone that survives death.
>
> **Parousia:** An event in Christianity that is also called The Second Coming. This is when Jesus will return in glory to judge the world.
>
> **Purgatory:** A place between heaven and hell where souls are purged, or cleansed, from sin so that they can enter heaven.

HINDUISM

Hinduism teaches that life and death are a constant cycle of birth, death and re-birth. This is known as **reincarnation**. A person's soul will live on earth many times and in different forms before reaching perfection and being released from this cycle.

The atman

Hindus believe that in every person there is an eternal soul known as the *atman*. Each person has a body, but the body changes, grows old and will eventually die. The *atman* is different as it lives on forever. It cannot be destroyed and never dies. When one body is worn out and dies, the *atman* is born again into a new life as a different person. Each *atman* can be re-born in many different lives, over hundreds and thousands of years. A Hindu scripture states:

> "As a person casts off worn-out clothes and puts on new ones, so does the *atman* cast off worn-out bodies and enter new ones."
> (Bhagavad Gita 2:22)

Karma

A good person earns good **karma** and a bad person earns bad *karma*. *Karma* is intentional action and it is carried over from one life to the next. People will not necessarily be rewarded or punished immediately, but it will happen at some time. Belief in *karma* gives Hindus the motivation to live a moral life and also explains the origin of evil and suffering. A person who has a difficult or miserable time in life is paying back for previous wrongdoing.

Moksha

Hindus believe that their ultimate aim is to escape from this cycle of being re-born over and over again. They hope one day to reach *moksha*. This is the name given to the freedom of the *atman* from the cycle of reincarnation. Hinduism teaches that there are many different ways to achieve *moksha*. One of them is through worship, and another is by trying to become wise. A Hindu funeral always involves cremation and many Hindus believe that sprinkling the ashes in the River Ganges will help a person achieve *moksha*. Hindus have different beliefs about what happens after *moksha*. Some Hindus say the *atman* is absorbed back into Brahman, the universal soul. Others believe the *atman* will be in the presence of Brahman after *moksha*, but the two will remain separate.

KEY TERMS

Reincarnation: The belief that after death a person's soul is reborn into a new body to live again.

Atman: The term used for the soul in Hinduism; the immortal part of a person that survives death.

Moksha: The final release of a soul from the cycle of reincarnation.

Karma: The result of a person's actions; the idea that every action, good or bad, will bring consequences.

ISLAM

Muslims use the Arabic word **Akhira** to refer to life after death. Every person has been created with free will and is responsible for their own actions. The judgement of Allah is final and will decide where a person spends eternity.

Judgement

Muslims believe that when they die, their body and soul will remain in **Barzakh**, a state of 'cold sleep', until the Day of Judgement. On this day, the end of time will be announced by the sound of a trumpet. The universe will be destroyed and everyone will be raised from their graves and brought before Allah to be judged. Muslims believe that each person has two recording angels, one for good deeds and one for bad deeds. Each angel writes down everything during a person's life. On the last day, the final record will be opened, and Allah will judge each person according to how they have lived. Those who God judges favourably will be rewarded with entry into **Jannah** (paradise). Those who have lived a life of sin will be sent to **Jahannam** (hell).

> "Indeed, those who disbelieve – never will their wealth or their children avail them against Allah at all, and those are the companions of the Fire; they will abide therein eternally." (Surah 3:116)

Heaven

Muslims believe people can never really understand what the afterlife will be like, but God has shown glimpses in the Qur'an, as outlined below. There is a complete balance between paradise and hell, as each time one is mentioned, a description of the other is given in contrast.

Jannah is a wonderful garden of everlasting peace and beauty, where true believers are rewarded by being at one with Allah. Families are reunited and there are constant pleasures without any pain. In *Jannah*, people rest on raised thrones, wearing beautiful clothes and precious jewels. Food and drink are served to people and are in constant supply. However, there are never feelings of drunkenness or having eaten too much. There is no pain or sorrow, hatred or anger, and Muslims will remain in this blissful place forever. The Qur'an describes *Jannah* as:

> "A beautiful place of final return – a garden of eternity whose doors will always be open to them." (Surah 38:49–50)

Jannah has eight gates through which believers can enter after their resurrection on Judgement Day. To enter through one of these gates, Muslims must have performed good deeds in their life, for example, being focused in prayer, giving to charity, or going on pilgrimage to Mecca.

Hell

People who have not followed God's wishes will go to *Jahannam*, or hell, where they will be punished. Hell is a place of torture, with unrelenting heat, fire and black smoke. It is for those people who have rejected the truth and done evil deeds. Just as the pleasures of paradise are real and experienced in a physical way, so too is the torment of hell. People will have a constant thirst, but the only drink is from a boiling spring. The food for the people in hell adds to the torment as it does not give any nourishment, nor does it stop hunger:

> "No food will there be for them except from a bitter, thorny plant which neither nourishes nor avails against hunger." (Surah 88:6–7)

Most Muslims believe that hell is eternal, with the torture lasting forever.

KEY TERMS

Akhira: The term used in Islam for life after death.

Barzakh: In Islam, this is the state of a person after they have died, while waiting for the final judgement at the end of time.

Jahannam: The term used in Islam for hell.

Jannah: The term used in Islam for paradise or heaven.

IN A GROUP

Study the artist's impressions below and on the next page.
How far do they match the beliefs of Christianity, Islam and Hinduism?

Last Judgement, Sistine Chapel, Rome – Michelangelo Buonarroti

Descent into Hell, from the Altarpiece of the Holy Sepulchre – Jaime Serra

The Heavenly Choir, a scene from Dante's *Paradiso* – Gustave Dore

Torture of the Fiery Rain, a scene from Dante's *Inferno* – Gustave Dore

FURTHER THINKING

Funeral rites are the customs and ceremonies that take place after a person has died.

Use the Internet to research the funeral rites in a religion of your choice. Explain how the funeral rites reflect this religion's teaching on life after death.

Non-religious views on the soul and the afterlife

Not all people who believe in life after death would call themselves 'religious'. Some people without any religious faith still believe that people have souls or spirits that continue after their physical death. For some people, near death experiences, paranormal experiences or witnessing ghosts convinces them that there is life beyond death. However, many non-religious people would maintain that death is the end of a person's existence and there is no evidence to suggest there is some form of afterlife.

KEY TERMS

Humanist: A person who believes that human experience and rational thinking, rather than religious teachings, provide a moral code to live by.

Atheist: A person who believes there are convincing reasons and arguments to conclude that God does not exist.

Paranormal: Events beyond the scope of normal scientific explanation, such as experiencing ghosts or the activity of spirits.

HUMANISM

Humanism cannot be described as a religion. It is more of a philosophy of life, or a 'life stance'. Humanists are atheists; therefore, they do not believe in any kind of afterlife. Humanists believe that when you die, you cease to exist. There is no reward or punishment for the way you have lived your life.

However, humanists do believe that there is a value in living an ethical lifestyle. If people have respect for themselves, others and the environment, then the world will be a better place for everyone. Living in a selfish way will not make a person happy and will cause unhappiness to others. It is best to live in a civilised way to get the most out of life while it lasts.

> "Reason, decency, tolerance, empathy and hope are human traits that we should aspire to, not because we seek reward of eternal life or because we fear the punishment of a supernatural being, but because they define our humanity." Jim Al-Khalili, President of the British Humanist Association.

ATHEISM

Atheists do not believe in God or any sort of spiritual realm. They deny the existence of life after death for the following reasons:

- Scientific evidence shows that when the body dies, everything decays.
- No one has returned from the dead to tell us.
- The end of life means exactly that, it is illogical to speak about life after death.
- Life-support machines prove that the brain dies before the rest of the body.

To an atheist, the only sort of afterlife a person has is how they live on in the memories of people who knew them when they were alive.

Case Study
Stephen Hawking

Stephen Hawking was a physicist who died in 2018, at the age of 76. However, he did not expect to see his 25th birthday, having been diagnosed with ALS, a disease which affects the nerve cells in the brain and spinal cord. He lived with the prospect of an early death for 49 years. In an interview shortly before he died, Hawking described his view of what happened to the brain and body after death:

> "I regard the brain as a computer which will stop working when its components fail. There is no heaven or afterlife for broken down computers; that is a fairy story for people afraid of the dark."

Hawking described himself as an atheist.

An Introduction to Philosophy of Religion

 IN A GROUP

Working in groups of 4 or 5, produce a poster showing each of your views about life after death. These views might not be the same.

QUESTIONS

1. (i) Name a religion that teaches that there is a final judgement. [1]
   (ii) Name a religion that teaches reincarnation. [1]
   (iii) What is meant by the term 'resurrection'? [1]
   (iv) What is meant by the term 'moksha'? [1]
   (v) Name one group that rejects the idea of life after death. [1]

2. Describe what one religion you have studied teaches about the afterlife. [5]

3. Explain why some people believe there is no life after death. [5]

4. "Belief in the afterlife provides comfort to someone who is suffering."
   Do you agree with this statement? Give reasons for your answer. [5]

5. "We cannot be certain what happens after death so we should just enjoy life."
   Do you agree or disagree? Give reasons for your answer showing that you have considered different points of view. [10]

 **IN A GROUP**

Discuss the following questions:
- How might each of the beliefs above help someone who mourning the death of a loved one?
- Are different religions simply different paths to the same goal?

Possible 'proofs' of life after death

Is there any evidence for an afterlife? Or is life after death a matter that depends on a person's personal beliefs? Some people have had out-of-the-ordinary experiences, which they claim can prove there is an afterlife. It can be difficult to establish whether these experiences are 'real' or the product of someone's imagination.

KEY TERMS

Hallucination: An experience involving the apparent perception of something that is not actually present at the time.

Illusion: A false belief that is not justified or warranted but which possesses a certain quality that suggests to some people that it is true.

Near death experience: An unusual experience that takes place as someone comes very close to dying. It usually involves some sort of 'out of the body' experience.

NEAR DEATH EXPERIENCES (NDEs)

This is an experience that has happened to someone who is very near death or who has been declared clinically dead. Such an experience might occur if someone has had a serious accident or is having an operation during which their heart has stopped beating, but the person has then been resuscitated and makes a recovery. Some people report a strange experience during the time when they were 'dead', which they claim is a glimpse of the afterlife. People who have had NDEs often describe similar experiences. Here are some of the things that people have reported following resuscitation:

"I saw a white light which became more and more intense. I was being drawn towards this light, which I associated with God."

"I knew I was drowning, and I felt my lungs fill with salt water. I then had the sensation of floating and suddenly I was looking down on my body as it sank further and further down."

"I felt that I was dead, and this was followed by the most pleasant feelings of peacefulness and calm."

"I was being drawn down a tunnel and moving at great speed."

"A beautiful garden appeared, and I saw my grandmother. She died when I was three years old, but I knew it was her. She was calling to me."

"I was floating towards a kaleidoscope of bright colours, when I heard a voice saying that it wasn't my time yet. I was suddenly back in my body on the operating table."

Having a near death experience usually has a profound effect on someone. For some people, a religious belief in the afterlife has been confirmed. They no longer fear death; they have a greater appreciation for the value of relationships with friends and family. Sometimes they have an increased desire for knowledge and learning. It is not just religious believers who have near death experiences. A person with no religious faith might turn to God after an experience.

Are near death experiences proof of an afterlife?

Near death experiences are often presented as evidence that the soul lives on after the body has died. Most commonly, people claim to have seen a glimpse of what heaven will be like. However, some people are very sceptical about whether NDEs are a glimpse of heaven, believing they are simply an illusion. Scientific and medical evidence can explain some aspects of NDEs, but they cannot account for all aspects of NDEs or the after effects. Some scientists are unwilling to dismiss the idea of a human soul and NDEs may be able to give insights into what happens when the physical body dies.

Some medical experts dismiss NDEs as hallucinations. Recent research suggests that there is a surge of electrical activity in the brain when a person is close to death, which could account for some of the experiences described by near-death survivors, such as the bright light. A sudden change in blood pressure could create a floating sensation. Some sceptics also claim that the descriptions of heaven are just what people would expect, so they are simply made up and unlikely to be real. Others have suggested that the peaceful and pleasant feelings are the body's way of making a person less afraid of dying.

Case Study
Ernest Hemingway

Ernest Hemingway (1899–1961) was an American writer who won the Nobel Prize in Literature in 1954. Some of his most popular books include *A Farewell to Arms* and *For Whom the Bell Tolls*. During the First World War, he was an ambulance driver for the American Red Cross. In 1918, he was wounded during fighting and had a near death experience. While he was recovering from his injury, he wrote a letter to his family, saying, "Dying is a very simple thing. I've looked at death and really I know." Years later, Hemingway explained to a friend what had occurred:

"A big Austrian trench mortar bomb, of the type that used to be called ash cans, exploded in the darkness. I died then. I felt my soul or something coming right out of my body, like you'd pull a silk handkerchief out of a pocket by one corner. It flew around and then came back and went in again and I wasn't dead anymore."

The near death experience affected Hemingway and influenced some of his writing. In *A Farewell to Arms*, the character Frederic Henry had an encounter with death and an experience similar to Hemingway's:

"There was a flash, as when a blast-furnace door is swung open, and a roar that started white and went red and on and on in a rushing wind. I tried to breathe but my breath would not come and I felt myself rush bodily out of myself and out and out and out and all the time bodily in the wind. I went out swiftly, all of myself, and I knew I was dead and that it had all been a mistake to think you just died. Then I floated, and instead of going on I felt myself slide back. I breathed and I was back."

REMEMBERING PAST LIVES

It is not just Hindus who believe in reincarnation. Some people with no religious faith claim they can remember past lives. Under hypnosis, people can often give descriptions of a former life, with accurate details from history, or about a place they have never visited. But are these experiences genuine? Some people would say they are just recounting details they have learnt from watching a documentary or reading a book that they had forgotten about. So, hypnosis has just re-awakened a past memory, not given a glimpse into a former life: their experience is nothing more than a fantasy or a delusion. However, other people claim such memories are genuine and can prove reincarnation.

Are remembered lives proof of an afterlife?

Some people, even those who do believe in reincarnation, are sceptical about whether past lives can be remembered. Many of the claims to remember a past life are the memories of children; it could be argued that children, especially the very young, have active imaginations and often invent imaginary friends or fantasy lives. People who claim to have remembered past lives could be making these stories up or hallucinating. However, there are some cases where there seems to be no logical explanation for a person's memories or behaviour, other than that they have lived a previous life.

IN A GROUP

Read the case study on the right and discuss the following questions:

- Do you think it is possible that people are reincarnated and can sometimes remember a past life?
- If so, do you think this could explain Dorothy Eady's experiences?
- If not, how would you explain her knowledge of ancient Egypt?
- Do you think people would have forgotten about Dorothy Eady by now if her story was made up?

Case Study
Dorothy Eady or Omm Seti

Dorothy Eady was born in London in 1904. At the age of three, she fell down some stairs and was found unconscious. The doctor declared her to be dead. However, an hour later she had recovered and was found playing in her bedroom with no sign of injury.

Shortly after the accident, she began to have dreams in which she saw a large building with columns and a garden with trees and flowers. She would often start crying and ask to be taken home. On one occasion, her parents took her to the British Museum. They went into the Egyptian galleries, with the exhibits of ancient mummies and statues of Egyptian gods and goddesses. Dorothy's parents were horrified when she began kissing the feet of the statues and demanding that she wanted to be left "with my people".

At the age of six, Dorothy said that hieroglyphic writing was familiar to her but that she had forgotten how to read it. At seven, she saw pictures of the temple of Seti I in Abydos, Egypt and said "This is my home! This is where I used to live. But where are all the gardens and trees?" As Dorothy grew up, her attitude towards Egyptian religion often got her into trouble. At school, there were Christian hymns that Dorothy refused to sing, and her Sunday School teacher asked her parents to keep her away from the class.

Finally, at the age of 27, Dorothy was able to go and live in Egypt. She married an Egyptian and obtained Egyptian citizenship. On arriving in Egypt, she knelt down and kissed the ground, announcing that she had come home to stay.

Dorothy believed that in a previous life she had been an Egyptian called Bentreshyt. After her mother died when she was very young, Bentreshyt became a temple priestess and took the vows to become a consecrated virgin at the age of twelve. However, she broke her vows and became pregnant, for which the punishment was death. Bentreshyt committed suicide rather than wait for the sentence to be carried out. Her lover was Pharaoh Seti I and their child would have been his successor.

After 19 years of living in Cairo, Dorothy decided to move to Abydos. At this time, local people started to call her Omm Seti, meaning 'Mother of Seti'. During one of her visits to the temple at Abydos, the chief inspector from the Egyptian Antiquities Department decided to check her knowledge. Dorothy proved she could identify all the wall paintings with what she remembered from her previous life. She was asked to work with Egyptologists and researchers who were investigating ancient Egypt. She was able to discover the garden at the temple of Seti I and her descriptions of the monuments and other things she saw during her previous life were repeatedly confirmed by the excavations of archaeologists. Many important discoveries were based on her memories from her past life.

Dorothy Eady died at the age of 81 and is buried in Abydos. There is still divided opinion as to whether she was the reincarnation of an Egyptian priestess or a liar with great acting skills. Perhaps everything was based on a dream she had as a child or maybe she had seen books and magazines about ancient Egypt. We may never know, but for many people this is one of the most fascinating cases of a possible reincarnation.

CHRISTIAN TEACHING ON THE RESURRECTION

Christians look to the resurrection of Jesus as proof of life after death. The Bible teaches that as God raised Jesus from the dead, those who have faith in him will also receive eternal life. For Christians, the resurrection proves that Jesus is God's Son and that God is faithful to the promises he has made. Belief in the resurrection of Jesus is a matter of faith and, like other miracles, cannot be scientifically proven. Over the years, alternative suggestions have been made in an attempt to explain the resurrection. For example:

- Someone else was crucified instead of Jesus.
- The disciples stole Jesus' body and pretended he had risen from the dead.
- Jesus wasn't dead when he was placed in the tomb. He was in a coma.

Christian teachers argue that none of these theories stands up to scrutiny. The Romans were experienced in carrying out crucifixions. They would not have made mistakes, such as executing the wrong person. They also checked to make sure that a prisoner really was dead before taking them down from the cross. Jesus' tomb was sealed with a large stone and there were Roman soldiers on guard. This was at the request of the religious leaders who were worried Jesus' disciples might steal the body, claiming there had been a resurrection. It would have been extremely difficult for Jesus' body to have been stolen, or for Jesus to have recovered and somehow escaped from the tomb. Finally, there is historical evidence that most of Jesus' followers were killed for their faith. Would they have been prepared to die for something they knew to be a lie?

Is the resurrection of Jesus proof of an afterlife?

Sceptics of the Gospel writers' accounts of the resurrection of Jesus say that there is no physical evidence for such an event, especially since it cannot happen anyway – people do not just come back from the dead after three days in a tomb. However, Jesus' followers did not expect him to be resurrected and they were astonished when the tomb was discovered empty. This was not what they expected to see. The Bible describes several post-resurrection appearances of Jesus to hundreds of witnesses. For Christians, the most obvious conclusion is that Jesus did rise from the dead, just as the Bible describes, proving there is an afterlife.

IN A GROUP

Working in groups of four:

- Two members decide on three arguments to say the resurrection did not happen.
- The other two come up with three arguments to say the resurrection happened as described in the Bible.

Present your arguments to each other and decide who has the most convincing case.

FURTHER THINKING

If the resurrection did not happen as described in the Bible, is it still possible for there to be life after death?

ACTIVITY

Construct a spider diagram or mind map to summarise the possible proofs for life after death.

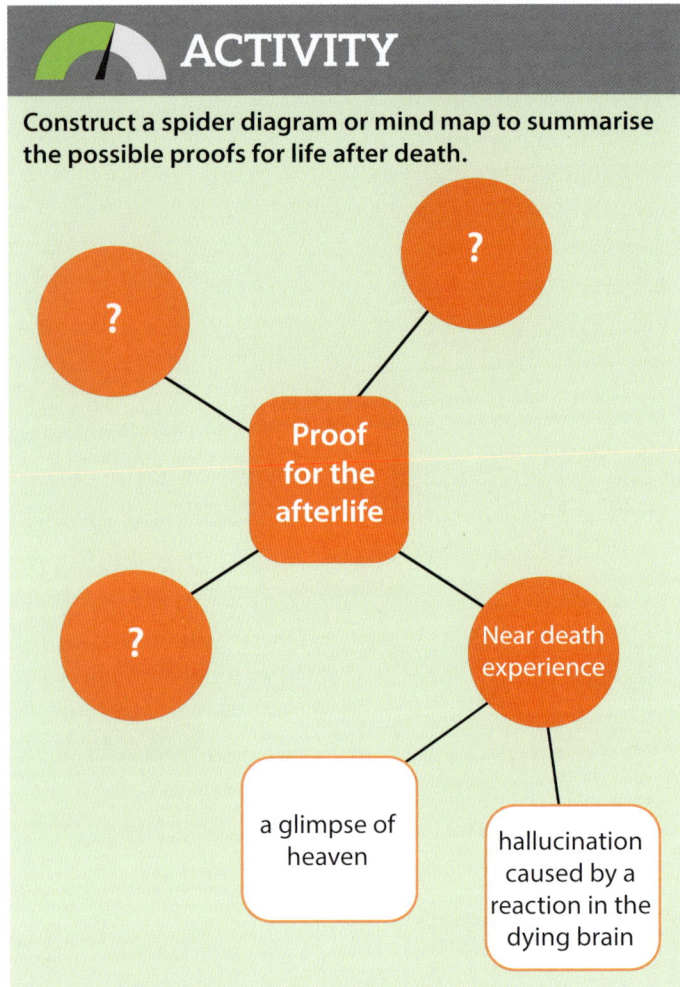

The impact of belief in the afterlife

Belief in the afterlife can affect the way believers live in this life:

- It provides a purpose to life.
- It encourages people to be disciplined and moral in their behaviour and show responsibility towards others.
- It can bring hope to people who are suffering in this life and provide comfort to those who are facing the death of someone close to them.
- It can give a sense of justice, through the reassurance that evil people will get what they deserve in the next life.

CHRISTIANITY

Belief in life after death is a very important part of the Christian faith. There is a very distinct relationship between life on Earth, judgement and the afterlife. According to Christianity, it is people's faith in God and their actions during their lives that determine how they are judged and where they will spend eternity. This has an impact on Christian behaviour, as they will try to live their lives in a moral way, according to God's laws, if they believe that one day God will hold them to account. Christians believe that they should recognise when they do wrong and confess to God in order to achieve forgiveness. All this gives a sense of purpose to people in their everyday lives. Belief in the afterlife can also help Christians cope with suffering and unfairness. It can reassure them that suffering is only temporary and evil people will be punished when they die.

HINDUISM

Hinduism teaches that the way people behave affects what will happen to them in the next life. Good deeds will bring rewards for the person who does them and bad actions will bring punishment. This is known as the law of *karma*. The punishment might take the form of being born into poverty in a future life and having to suffer, or even reincarnated as a plant or animal if a soul has repeatedly failed to learn lessons in human form. Therefore, Hindus do what they can to build up good *karma* in this life to ensure a better experience in the next life. They worship God, are kind to others and practice meditation as a spiritual discipline. Hindus believe it is especially important to avoid any violent actions, as violence generates more violence. Living good lives will ultimately lead to *moksha*, the final goal of all Hindus.

ISLAM

Muslims believe that a person has only one chance to live their life and will be judged on how they live it. Life on Earth is a preparation for life after death. A person's behaviour now will directly affect his or her afterlife. Muslims believe they will be judged according to how well they have followed the teachings of the Qur'an and the example of Muhammad. Everyone has free will and is responsible for their actions. Muslims try to live the whole of their lives in submission to Allah, aware that every action is recorded. They believe that religious duties include faith, worship and helping others who are less fortunate. The promise of eternal life can help to motivate good deeds and generosity, as these will be rewarded in paradise.

QUESTIONS

1. Describe some of the features of a near death experience. [5]
2. Outline the arguments a person might use to prove there is life after death. [5]
3. Explain what one religion you have studied teaches about resurrection. [5]
4. "Knowing there is an afterlife can reassure believers that God is always just."
   Do you agree with this statement? Give reasons for your answer. [5]
5. "It is better to focus on this life rather than the afterlife."
   Do you agree with this statement? Give reasons for your answer. [5]
6. "Without belief in the afterlife there is very little motivation to do good."
   Do you agree or disagree? Give reasons for your answer showing that you have considered different points of view. [10]

LEARNING OUTCOMES

Learning outcome	Know & understand	Need to revise	Completed
The teachings of world religions on the afterlife • Christianity • Hinduism • Islam			
Non-religious views on the soul and the afterlife • Humanism • Atheism			
Possible 'proofs' of life after death • Near death experiences • Remembering past lives • To what extent these experiences are proofs of an afterlife			
The impact of belief in the afterlife • Christianity • Hinduism • Islam			

Glossary

Afterlife: The belief in life after death.

Agnostic: A person who is uncertain whether or not God exists because there is insufficient evidence.

Akhira: The term used in Islam for life after death.

Atheist: A person who believes that there are convincing reasons and arguments to conclude that God does not exist.

Atman: The term used for the soul in Hinduism; the immortal part of a person that survives death.

Attribute: A quality or feature that is regarded as a characteristic or inherent part of someone or something.

Avatar: The term used in Hinduism for a god on Earth in the form of a human or animal.

Barzakh: In Islam, this is the state of a person after they have died, while waiting for the final judgement at the end of time.

Belief: This is something that people accept to be true or exists when they may not necessarily have proof.

Big Bang theory: A scientific theory that seeks to provide an explanation for the origins of the universe by reference to an initial 'explosion.'

Brahma: The Hindu god in control of creating.

Brahman: Many Hindus believe Brahman is the one supreme God, seen in many different forms.

Conversion: The process of a person changing from one belief/religion to another, e.g. someone who changes from being a Muslim to a Christian.

Creationism: The belief that God created the world as outlined in a sacred text such as the book of Genesis in the Bible. It is sometimes interpreted to denote rejection of evolution.

Design argument: An argument that claims the existence of God can be inferred from the intricate design and complexity of the world in which people live. Also known as the teleological argument.

Devil/Satan: A term used to describe a personal, spiritual adversary of God, whose aim is to thwart God's purpose and plans.

Enlightenment: The state of having knowledge, wisdom or awakened intellect; Buddhists believe a person can become enlightened by following the teachings of the Buddha.

Eternal: Something that is everlasting and with no beginning or end. Theists often describe God as eternal.

Evolution: A scientific theory that claims that human life developed from simple organisms through natural selection.

Existence: The state or fact of existing. This term is frequently used when talking about God.

Fall, The: The disobedience of Adam and Eve, resulting in their expulsion from the Garden of Eden.

First Cause argument: The theory that everything has a cause apart from God, who is the first cause, the 'uncaused'. This theory is used to argue in support of the existence of God. Also known as the cosmological argument.

Free will: The belief that God has given each person the power to perform actions for which he or she is fully responsible; the ability to choose and act on the basis of one's freedom. Christians and Muslims believe that God created humans with free will.

Galaxy: A cluster of billions of stars, held together by gravity.

General revelation: Knowledge of God available to everyone, e.g. through reflection on nature.

Genesis: The first book of the Bible, which includes the Christian creation story of God being the one who made the world we live in.

Hallucination: An experience involving the apparent perception of something that is not actually present at the time.

Holy: The word used in the original Hebrew scriptures that means 'separate' or 'set apart'.

Holy Spirit: The third person of the Trinity; a gift to believers in the early church at Pentecost. The Holy Spirit guides and empowers Christians today.

Humanist: A person who believes that human experience and rational thinking, rather than religious teachings, provide a moral code to live by.

Illusion: A false belief that is not justified or warranted but which possesses a certain quality that suggests to some people that it is true.

Immanent: The belief that God is involved and present in his creation.

Impersonal: The idea that God does not possess personal qualities and does not enter into personal relationships with individuals.

Jahannam: The term used in Islam for hell.

Jannah: The term used in Islam for paradise or heaven.

Karma: The result of a person's actions; the idea that every action, good or bad, will bring consequences.

Knowable: The idea that believers can have a personal relationship with God, who is described as a father or friend.

Miracle: An extraordinary event that cannot be explained by natural or scientific laws. It is usually regarded as a direct action of God and provides evidence for his existence.

Moksha: The final release of a soul from the cycle of reincarnation.

Monotheism: The belief in one God.

Moral argument: An argument for the existence of God, based on the idea that all people have an instinctive sense of right and wrong that comes from God.

Moral evil: Suffering or pain caused by the acts/words/choices of another person, e.g. murder.

Natural selection: The process through which living organisms adapt and change.

Natural suffering / natural evil: Suffering or pain caused by nature, e.g. earthquakes, volcanoes and floods.

Near death experience: An unusual experience that takes place as someone comes very close to dying. It usually involves some sort of 'out of the body' experience.

Numinous: Having a deeply religious or spiritual experience, sometimes triggered by being in a particular place or situation.

Omnibenevolent: All-good; it is a quality essential to the nature of God. God is totally loving and the source of all goodness.

Omnipotent: All-powerful; it is a quality essential to the nature of God. There is nothing that is beyond God or impossible for him to do.

Omnipresent: Present everywhere. It is an attribute of God.

Omniscient: All-knowing; a quality essential to the nature of God.

Original Sin: The Christian teaching that everyone is born sinful, with an inclination to do evil. Original Sin is the result of Adam and Eve's disobedience to God.

Paranormal: Events beyond the scope of normal scientific explanation, such as experiencing ghosts or the activity of spirits.

Parousia: An event in Christianity that is also called The Second Coming. This is when Jesus will return in glory to judge the world.

Personal: Having personal qualities and the ability to interact with others.

Polytheism: The belief in the existence of many gods. It is viewed by many as the opposite of monotheism.

Prayer: A way in which people communicate with God either personally or as a group.

Purgatory: A place between heaven and hell where souls are purged, or cleansed, from sin so that they can enter heaven.

Ramayana: A Hindu scripture, telling the story of Rama and Sita.

Reason: The power to determine truth by rational means.

Red-shift: The change in wavelength of light from a star as it moves away from Earth.

Reincarnation: The belief that after death a person's soul is reborn into a new body to live again.

Religious experience: An experience that is caused by God rather than by ordinary or natural processes. Religious believers argue that a miracle is a type of religious experience. Also known as a spiritual experience.

Resurrection: The act of being raised from the dead. In Christianity, this refers to the resurrection of Jesus by God and also the resurrection of believers to eternal life.

Sacrament: An outward and visible sign of a deeper spiritual reality. Sacraments are practised in Protestant and Catholic Churches, e.g. baptism and communion.

Sacred texts: A holy document used by a religion, e.g. the Bible, which is inspired by God and believed by Christians to be the final and ultimate source of authority.

Scripture: The holy writings of a religious group which contain guidelines and instructions for living.

Shiva: The Hindu god in control of destroying what needs to be replaced.

Special revelation: Knowledge of God that is not available to everyone, but rather to an individual or a group of people. Dreams, visions, prophecies and miracles can all be regarded as special revelation by Christians. Reading the Bible is also special revelation when a believer feels God is speaking specifically to them.

Soul: The spiritual or immaterial part of a human being that continues to exist after a person has died. The soul is the essential part of someone that survives death.

Tawhid: The term used to describe the oneness of God in Islam.

Theist: A person who believes in the existence of God.

Theistic argument: A religious argument claiming there is evidence for the existence of God.

Theistic evolution: The belief that God controls evolution, as he created a world that could change and develop.

Transcendence: Comes from the Latin prefix trans meaning beyond. The belief that God is beyond and not limited by the world that he created.

Trinity: The Christian belief that God can exist in three persons – Father, Son and Holy Spirit.

Trimurti: The term referring to the three most important Gods in Hinduism – Brahma, Vishnu and Shiva.

Unknowable: The belief that God is beyond human understanding and humans can never hope to know and understand him completely.

Vishnu: The Hindu god in control of preserving and sustaining everything.

Vision: Something that is seen in a dream or dream-like state and regarded by the subject as a revelation from God.

Worship: A religious act of adoration; where people are freely expressing and acknowledging the worth of God.

Copyright

Unless otherwise stated below, all photographs are ©iStockPhoto.

Art Archive: page 30, top right; page 68, both.

US Library of Congress: page 50, right. Mother Teresa and Archbishop John J. O'Connor in NYC [New York], 15 October 1984, Bernard Gotfryd photograph collection (Library of Congress) Reproduction Number: LC-DIG-gtfy-04162

Alistair Anderson: page 30, bottom left.

Nicky Cruz: page 57.

Extract on page 38: NIGHT by Elie Wiesel. Copyright © 1972, 1985 by Elie Wiesel. English translation Copyright © 2006 by Marion Wiesel. (Hill and Wang, 2006) Originally published as La Nuit by Les Editions de Minuit. Copyright © 1958 by Les Editions de Minuit. Used by permission of Georges Borchardt, Inc., for Les Editions de Minuit.

Glossary: most entries are either ©CCEA or are adapted from CCEA material.

Index

Aberfan Disaster 44
African Traditional Religion 35
Afterlife 8, 66–77
Agnostic 7–8, 9, 10, 12, 16
Akhira 68, 69
Al-Ghazali, Abu Hamid 40, 41
Aquinas, Thomas 9, 10
Argument
    First Cause (Cosmological) 9, 10, 13, 15
    From Design (Teleological) 10–12, 13, 15, 22, 60
    From Religious Experience 10, 13–14
    Moral 10, 15–16
Atheist 7, 8, 10, 12, 16, 17, 42, 43, 59, 60, 71
Atman 20, 23, 24, 34, 46, 53, 67, 68
Augustine, St 39, 57, 59
Avatar 34, 35

Bacon, Francis 10, 13
Barzakh 68, 69
Bely, Jean-Pierre 61
Big Bang Theory 10, 11, 23–24
Buddha, The 14, 46, 47
Brahma 19, 23, 34, 35
Brahman 19, 20, 31, 32, 34, 53, 54, 55, 68

Cosmological Argument (see Argument, From Design)
Copernicus, Nicholaus 20
Creation
    Christianity 18
    Hinduism 19–20
    Judaism 18
Creationism 18, 23
Cruz, Nicky 16, 57

Darwin, Charles 11, 20, 21–23
Design, Argument From (see Argument, From Design)
Devil 7, 38–39
Dunblane Primary School 44

Eady, Dorothy 74–75
Enlightenment 46, 47
Epicurus 42, 43
Evil and Suffering 37–47, 67
Evolution 7, 11, 12, 16, 20, 21–23, 60
Existence of God 7–25, 42–43, 46, 64

First Cause Argument (see Argument, First Cause)
Four Noble Truths 46

Free Will 38, 39, 68, 77
Freud, Sigmund 10, 14, 15, 62–63
Friedman, Alexander 23

Genesis 18, 20, 22, 23, 24, 38, 39
Gandhi, Mahatma 53–54
God's Providence 45

Hallucination 62, 63, 72, 73, 74
Hawking, Stephen 71
Healing on the Streets (HOTS) 58
Heaven 67, 68, 69, 73
Hemingway, Ernest 73
Hell 67, 68, 69
Hick, John 41, 45
Holy Spirit 27, 32, 33–34, 49, 51, 63
Hubble, Edwin 24
Humanist 8, 71
Human Suffering 37–47
Hume, David 9, 12, 60
Huxley, Thomas Henry 7

Illusion 14, 63, 72, 73
Immanence 27, 32
Inconsistent Triad 42
Innocent Suffering 44
Irenaeus 41

Jahannam 68, 69
Jannah 68–69
Judgement, Final 66–67, 68–69

Kant, Immanuel 14, 15, 16
Karma 20, 46, 47, 67–68, 76
Knock Shrine 61
Knowable God 27, 29, 31–32

Lemaitre, Georges-Henri 23
Lewis, CS 39, 44, 57
Lisbon Earthquake 45
Lourdes 61, 62
Lyell, Charles 20–22

McLoughlin, Mary 60
Mill, John Stuart 43
Miracles 59–61
Moksha 34, 68, 77
Monotheism 7, 31, 33–34

Moral Argument (see Argument, Moral)
Moral Evil 37, 43
Mother Teresa 50
Muhammad 14, 32, 35, 51, 52, 57, 61, 62, 77

Natural Evil/Suffering 37, 43
Natural Selection 21–22
Nature of God 27–35, 50
Near Death Experience (NDE) 72–73
Nietzsche, Friedrich 43
Newman, Cardinal John 14, 15
Newton, Isaac 9, 11
Numinous 61–62, 63

Omm Seti (Eady, Dorothy) 74–75
Omnibenevolent 11, 27, 28, 35, 42, 43, 45, 59
Omnipotent 10, 11, 27, 28, 31, 42, 43, 45, 51, 52, 59
Omnipresent 27, 28, 34, 35, 52, 54
Omniscient 11, 27, 28, 45
Origin of Species 21
Otto, Rudolf 60, 62

Paley, William 9, 11, 60
Parousia 66–67
Past Lives 74
Personal God (see Knowable God)
Plotinus 41
Polytheism 7, 31, 35, 52
Prayer 27, 32, 49, 51, 52, 53, 54, 55, 56, 58, 59, 62, 63, 69
    Answered 13, 17, 32, 33, 50, 56, 58–59
    Unanswered 58–59
Problem of Evil 37–47
Puja 54
Purgatory 67

Ramayana 34, 35, 53
Reincarnation 20, 34, 40, 46, 47, 53, 67, 68, 74, 76
Religious Experience (see Argument, From Religious Experience)
Religious Experience Research Centre 14
Religious Truth 25, 42
Resurrection 66, 67, 75
Revelation 55–64
    General 55, 56
    Special 55, 56
Russell, Bertrand 10, 14

Sacred Texts, Christianity 18, 49–50, 57–58
Sacred Texts, Hinduism 53
Sacred Texts, Islam 51–52, 57
Satan (see Devil)
Science And Religion 25
Scientific Truth 23, 25
Shiva 19, 34, 35
Shruti 53
Smith, William 20
Smriti 53
Soubirous, Bernadette 61
Soul 66, 67, 68, 71, 73
Suffering (see Evil and Suffering)
Swinbourne, Richard 10, 13

Tawhid 35
Teleological Argument (see Argument, From Design)
Theist 7, 8, 16
Theistic Evolution 21, 23
Theodicies 40
Toronto Blessing 63
Transcendence 27, 31–32
Trimurti 34, 35
Trinity 33–34

Unknowable God 7, 27, 30, 31–32
Upanishads, The 53

Vedas, The 19, 53
Vishnu 19, 23, 34, 35
Visions 27, 55, 56, 61, 62

Wiesel, Elie 38,
Wesley, John 58
Wilson, Edward Osborne 14, 15
Wilson, Gordon 47
Wish-Fulfillment 62–63
Woolston, Thomas 59, 60
Worship, Christianity 51
Worship, Hinduism 54
Worship, Islam 52